Teenagers &Alcohol

When Saying No Isn't Enough

Roger E. Vogler, PhD
and Wayne R. Bartz, PhD

The Charles Press, Publishers
Philadelphia

Copyright © 1992 by The Charles Press, Publishers, Inc.
All rights reserved.

The Charles Press, Publishers
Post Office Box 15715
Philadelphia, PA 19103

Library of Congress Cataloging-in-Publication Data

Vogler, Roger E.
    Teenagers and alcohol / Roger E. Vogler and Wayne R. Bartz.
    p.   cm.
    Includes bibliographical references.
    ISBN 0-914783-57-2
    1. Teenagers —United States—Alcohol use. 2. Alcoholism—United States—
Prevention. I. Bartz, Wayne R., 1938-   . II. Title.
HV5135.V65 1991   91-38965
362.29′22′0835—dc20   CIP

Printed in the United States of America

ISBN 0-914783-57-2

We respectfully dedicate this book to
Mothers Against Drunk Driving (MADD)
and to
Students Against Driving Drunk (SADD)
for their unflagging commitment
to saving innocent lives.

Acknowledgments

We are grateful to the following people who read a draft of this book and gave us valuable feedback for improvement: Dr. Ray Barnett, Dr. Roger Morgan, Dr. Dick Rasor, Dr. Nancy Webber and Dr. Ted Weissbach. Thanks also to Linda Hamel, JD and Fred Vogler, MA for technical assistance.

Contents

Introduction

Have you ever found yourself in any of the following situations?

- You go into your teenager's bedroom to collect dirty clothes and discover a half-empty bottle of vodka in the back of the closet.

- You return home unexpectedly and to everyone's surprise find your teenager and a few friends drinking wine coolers in the kitchen.

- You are watching television, sipping a drink, and your 11-year-old says, "That looks good." Your 13-year-old chimes in, "Yeah, how come you can drink and we can't?"

- The father of one of your boy's best friends calls you and says that your son and his son were together last night drinking beer. His son threw up after he got home and confessed that they had had a twelvepack and drank most of it in a theater parking lot.

- Your teenage daughter tells you about a party some high school friends are planning. She is unable, however, to assure you that alcohol will not be served and is vague about who is coming and whether any adults will be present.

- Until recently your teenage son has been a well-behaved, good student. Over the past few months his grades have slipped, he avoids contact with you and he has not been responsive to your family's rules. You wonder if alcohol has anything to do with it.

- It's late on a weekend night. You and your spouse are getting ready for bed and you hear your daughter go quickly to her room without saying her usual goodnight to you. You knock and upon entering her bedroom, you immediately smell alcohol.

- You are out at a restaurant and are drinking beer with your dinner when your 12-year-old says, "Dad, you're drinking beer and pretty soon you'll be driving us home. Our teacher says you should never drink and drive."

- Your teenage daughter tells you with obvious concern that her friend had opened a beer in the back seat of her car while she was driving the other day. She asks you how she should handle it if it happens again.

- You and your spouse enjoy moderate drinking. Your kids have recently become vocally critical and righteously indignant whenever you have a drink and the situation has become increasingly unpleasant.

- Your brother Ted and his wife Janet are coming over for dinner. They always bring along a couple of bottles of wine and Ted typically ends up drinking most of it. Your daughter asks, "How come Uncle Ted always gets so silly when they eat here? Last time he ended up crying."

- Your 19-year-old son — who you have never seen drink before — comes home for vacation from college. You find him sitting in the backyard, reading the newspaper and casually drinking a beer.

- Your 9-year-old daughter accidentally picks up your glass of whiskey and takes a drink. She runs to the bathroom, spits it out, returns with a red face — obviously upset — and asks angrily, "Why would you drink something that tastes so awful?"

- Your son's best high school friend has the reputation of being a "party-animal," and his parents do not seem to be aware or perhaps are not concerned about his drinking. You are worried that your son will be tempted to follow his friend's example.

- It's barbecue time, the afternoon is beautiful and your guests are enjoying themselves immensely. Most of the adults are drinking beer and you notice that one of them has given his pre-teen daughter a small glass of beer. Upon seeing this your daughter asks you, "Can I have some too?"

- You usually drink two drinks every night but have recently cut back. Just as was the case when you were dieting, you feel a little irritable about depriving yourself. You are usually quite playful with your son during cocktail hour and he senses your mood difference. He asks why you don't have a drink.

- Sandra, your 17-year-old daughter, has been doing well in school, has always been well-behaved and responsible, and you have never had to worry a great deal about her. Her younger brother who is sometimes chided for not being as responsible as his older sister, tells you, "You always think Sandy's such an angel, but she's not! You don't even know that she and her friends are called 'The Alkies' by everybody at school!"

- At a party you spot your 10-year-old son slyly sipping a drink that someone has left on a table.

- The police call you at 3 in the morning and say they have your son down at the police station. He had been arrested for drunk driving.

- As you polish off your third drink before dinner you notice that your daughter is watching with obvious curiosity and a questioning expression. You ask her why the quizzical look and she just says "No reason," turns and walks out of the room. You wonder about the kind of effect your drinking might be having on your kids, but find it easier to let the opportunity to discuss it with her pass than to confront the situation.

Kids learn about alcohol and drinking every day from experiences like those described above. Although teachers, friends and relatives have an effect on children's attitudes and decisions about drinking, the parents' role is critical and influential. The focus of this book is how to best use that parental influence. We suggest ways to develop a relationship with your child that will maximize your influence. We offer the latest scientific information about alcohol and carefully consider the pros and cons of drinking. We discourage the use of alcohol for those under 21 years of age. For teens who don't drink or are tentative about trying alcohol, we provide a rational argument for not becoming a drinker. But many young people do drink and we are realistic about this. The majority of teenagers have already tried alcohol and many drink regularly. Some of them already have a drinking problem, even some *very* young people. We must deal with these realities to reduce the hazards and the all too frequent tragedies resulting from teenage drinking. Parents and concerned others usually do the best they can and we sympathize with their worries and frustrations about what more they can do to help.

Conventional wisdom provides little help to parents; its emphasis is on enforcing the same rules about drinking we learned as children, using scare tactics or the "Just Say No!" approach. These methods only work for some teenagers. Many others do not respond to any intervention despite major efforts by their parents. But the worst thing parents can do is nothing. Rather than watching helplessly from the sidelines with fingers crossed in worried frustration, reading this book will provide parents with the tools necessary to take an active role in guiding their children toward making responsible choices about alcohol.

PART 1

Preparing for Action

Parents have good reason to worry about their teenagers drinking. No teen is immune to the influence of an alcohol-oriented society—which ours most certainly is—and parents are not doing their job if they simply ignore the potential problem and "hope for the best." Great expectations were pinned on school drug and alcohol education programs during the '80s, but parents were largely uninvolved and despite great expense and effort, the results have been discouraging. "Just Say No!" approaches were widely promoted, but again the results were very disappointing. Still, it is not necessary to throw up our hands in despair; we are far from helpless. Actively involved parents *can* do a great deal and the payoffs are well worth the effort.

The program we propose has nine steps. The first three steps (discussed in Part 1) are understanding the problem, getting the facts about alcohol and learning how to maximize parental influence. We will describe the scope of teenage drinking problems and come to some understanding of what has been tried and which methods have proved to be dead-ends. The basic facts about alcohol are presented to lay the groundwork for informed, meaningful parental involvement in teenage drinking decisions. We then spell out some sound, proven principles that can help parents build the kind of relationship that enhances their influence on their children's ultimate decisions about alcohol.

Step 1

Understanding the Problem

Former Senator Howard Baker likes to tell the story about a congressman who received the following letter:

Dear Congressman:

How do you stand on whiskey?

The congressman, uncertain of the position of the concerned voter, framed the following reply:

My Dear Friend:

I had not intended to discuss this controversial subject at this particular time. However, I want you to know that I do not shun a controversy. On the contrary, I will take a stand on any issue at any time, regardless of how fraught with controversy it may be. You have asked me how I feel about whiskey. Here is how I stand on this issue.

If, when you say whiskey, you mean the Devil's Brew; the poison scourge; the bloody monster that defiles innocence, dethrones reason, destroys the home, creates misery, poverty, fear, literally takes the bread from the mouths of little children; if you mean the evil drink that topples the Christian man and woman from the pinnacles of righteous, gracious living into the bottomless pit of degradation and despair, shame and helplessness and hopelessness, then certainly, I am against it with all my power.

But if, when you say whiskey, you mean the oil of conversation, the philosophic wine, the ale that is consumed when great fellows get together, that puts a song in their hearts and laughter on their lips, and the warm glow of contentment in their eyes; if you mean Christmas cheer; if you mean the stimulating drink that puts the spring in the old gentleman's step on a frosty morning; if you mean the drink that enables the man to magnify his joy and his happiness and to forget, if only for a little while, life's great tragedies and heartbreaks and sorrows. If you mean that drink the sale of which pours into our Treasury untold millions of dollars which are used to provide tender care for little crippled children, our blind, our deaf, our pitiful aged and infirm; to build highways, hospitals and schools, then certainly I am in favor of it.

This is my stand, and I will not compromise.

                                                           Your Congressman

This waffling letter highlights the many conflicts regarding the role of alcohol in our society. Is it "The Great Gift of God," as Puritan minister Cotton Mather described it, or rather "The Devil's Scourge"? Should it be readily available or illegal? Cheap or expensive? When key figures gathered not long ago in Washington to officially inaugurate the government's multi-billion-dollar "War on Drugs," the meeting was followed by a cocktail party during which success in the "War" was toasted with champagne. One thing is clear: as a society we do not now, nor have we ever, agreed about the pros and cons of alcohol.

Whatever our personal opinion, we must acknowledge that teens and alcohol are well acquainted. During the past decade the percentage of high school seniors who have tried alcohol has remained constant at 92 percent. Only eight out of one hundred 18 year olds would claim they have never taken a drink. There has been enormous public concern about the hazards of illicit drugs, but alcohol remains by far the number one problem for teenagers. It is important for parents to realize that no matter what their child's upbringing, no matter what the parents' drinking habits may be and no matter what programs are offered in school, nearly all kids are going to try drinking at one time or another. The notion that children can be protected or somehow immunized from alcohol until age 21 is untrue and anyone who believes this is simply not in touch with the facts. If teens are going to make their own decisions about drinking—and ultimately they will—parents need to do whatever they can to maximize their input.

Fortunately, teens often want their parents' input; a recent Gallup poll reported that 39 percent of all teens feel the need to talk with their parents about drinking. Parents can definitely influence their children's decisions and they can actively inspire them *not* to drink. Or, if young adults already do drink, parents can help them learn to do so in the safest, most sensible way. Teaching parents how to maximize their parental input and influence is the primary goal of this book.

The logical first step is to consider the most up-to-date information available on teen drinking. Should parents be worried? No debate here; there is plenty to be concerned about. Sixty percent of high school seniors are regular drinkers (have used alcohol in the past 30 days) and among those, half of them drink heavily on occasion and nearly one-third see no great risk in having four or five drinks every day. In addition, one out of three high school seniors report that most or all of their friends get drunk at least once a week. Finally, one out of every ten young people has used alcohol as a preteen (i.e., before the seventh grade).

A few years ago the director of a local drug abuse program in California proclaimed: "I think 85 percent of all high school kids abuse alcohol, because there's no such thing as using alcohol intelligently for those under 21." Must we conclude, then, that 92 percent of high school seniors today are "alcohol abusers"? Hardly. The best available current data indicate that over the past decade there have been significant changes in adolescent alcohol use and these changes have been for the better. For example, the proportion of seniors who are current drinkers fell from a high of over 72 percent in 1978 to 64 percent in the late 1980s and to just over 60 percent by 1990. The typical quantity of alcohol consumed by teens who drink has dropped by 11 percent and the number who admit to drinking daily (4 percent) is 40 percent lower than figures obtained in the late 1970s. These declining teen alcohol use figures parallel an overall decline in the amount of drinking by adults too, both perhaps the result of a growing societal push for better health and moderation in all things.

Taking an overview, then, the current statistical picture reflects great variation in the amount that teenagers drink, when they drink and with whom they drink, just as is the case with adults. If

parents react to each instance of teen drinking as if it were some kind
of disturbed or delinquent behavior, they are only missing opportunities to establish meaningful interaction and exert positive influence on their kids. Ignoring the behavior is also irresponsible.
Donna Shalala, president of the University of Wisconsin, was
interviewed by *Time* magazine early in 1990. She specified drinking
as the biggest problem on college campuses today. Dr. Shalala
observes that society did indeed change the legal drinking age to
21, but in so doing failed to really consider what actually goes on at
most colleges; college social life is traditionally oriented around
drinking, whether it occurs at local taverns or in fraternity houses.

> ...young people are drinking in junior high school and high school.
> They get to the university and we're saying, Hey, you can't drink.
> Some of it is unrealistic.... Young people are paying almost no
> attention to the law. They're still getting access to alcohol.

These facts must be faced: 92 percent of our children are
going to try alcohol before they finish high school; nearly two-
thirds of this group will probably become regular drinkers while
they are still in high school and this picture is not likely to change
or go away in the near future. Parents have two choices: (1)they
can avoid the issue altogether and hope that their children do not
get in trouble with alcohol, or (2) they can take an active role by
getting involved—the earlier the better—by teaching their kids
what they need to know about alcohol in order to make an
intelligent decision to drink or not to drink. If parents choose this
latter alternative they must make sure that they are involved in
the decision-making process from the start when children are still
open to suggestion from their parents.

Most parents are woefully unprepared when it comes to
discovering and learning how to deal with teenage drinking. Consider the distressing situation of Ruth and Lloyd Perkins, a happily
married couple in their late 30s. They have two teenage children—
Jeff, who is 15, and Julie, 17. They are good kids who have generally
been trouble-free other than minor scrapes; they've done well in
school and enjoy a wide circle of social contacts. One Friday night
Jeff came home a little later than usual and slipped quietly into the
bathroom, stayed about 20 minutes, then emerged looking a little

worse for wear. His mother immediately asked him if he was OK and expressed concern about the possibility of his having the flu. His response suggested that he was *not* all right and that it had nothing to do with the flu. He was obviously drunk. His father got wind of what was going on and began loudly interrogating Jeff and berating him: "Where were you tonight? Who were you with? You know I have told you never to drink! What in the world's the matter with you?" Realizing how angry her husband was, Ruth intervened and got Jeff off to bed. The Perkinses sat in silence for a while, dismayed to think that their son would drink alcohol after they had made it so clear that drinking was not acceptable until he turned 21, at which time he could legally make his own decision. The next morning they sat down with Jeff to discuss the situation. Jeff knew they were angry and upset and he listened to several detailed restatements of the family rules about not drinking. His parents emphasized the hazards of drinking: the risk to his schoolwork; the risk of having an accident while driving when drunk; perhaps not being able to run on the track team; damage to his health and the effect on his family's reputation. Jeff defended himself by claiming that someone else had bought the liquor, that at the beginning of the evening he was the only one not drinking and that his curiosity had gotten the best of him. He admitted that his willpower had finally broken down and that he began to drink even though he didn't really want to at the time. He said that he was sorry, knew that he had been wrong and swore that it would never happen again. After a bit more discussion everybody calmed down and Mr. and Mrs. Perkins reminded Jeff how much they loved and cared about him and that they didn't want anything bad to happen. A few tears and bear hugs later, things returned to normal around the Perkins household.

All went well for about four months and then there was another incident. This time Jeff did not come home sick, but when he entered the house, his parents were still awake and it was immediately apparent to them that he was drunk—his slurred speech and silly comments were an instant give-away. This time his parents were even more upset than before because they thought that the problem was dealt with once and for all. They were sure that Jeff had understood the importance of not drinking and he had promised them that he would never do it again. End of problem...or so they thought.

Variations on the Perkins' unhappy situation are experienced by concerned and caring parents every day. What went wrong? In part, the Perkinses failed to understand that even when children have a clear intellectual understanding of the rules and a sincere intention to follow them, it does not mean that those rules will always be followed. Many parents truly believe that if their kids just understand the hazards of underage drinking and that their family does not want them to drink, they won't. "But I explained it to him and he understood it! He knows I love him and he has always been a good kid. I just don't get it!" However, for a variety of reasons, understanding and good explanations are often not enough. For one, young people are profoundly influenced by people other than their parents, particularly by their peers. At one time or another all kids will find themselves with the opportunity to drink and will be exposed to situations where drinking will play an important role in "fitting in." Simply being aware of their family's rules about alcohol and attempting to maintain a "good" conscience clearly are not strong enough negative influences to stop most teenagers from drinking. It is especially hard for young adults because they now are being presented with a whole new set of peer group rules that *encourage* drinking. We know that fitting in is of great importance to young people and that they will often do just about anything to ensure this. As well, drinking is inherently pleasurable for most people, so it is not exactly a hard task or a great sacrifice to engage in if it means "fitting in."

In an earlier era, "Just Say No!" may have had a big impact on a significant number of young people. This is less true today, perhaps because parental authority and the sanctity of parental opinions is not what it used to be. Keep in mind that our young people are being exposed to an ever-widening diversity of opinions, ideas and models. They are being taught to think for themselves, to question and consider alternative viewpoints and to reach conclusions on their own. In fact, "critical thinking" has become a catchword in education (and many educators and social philosophers believe this is an essential skill if we are to survive as a nation in the highly competitive 21st century). Youngsters have naturally become less inclined to accept "rules" without question, regardless of who tries to impose these rules. In addition, as they approach adulthood, they face the ambiguous status of becoming "legal adults" at age 18—qualified to die for their country, vote, live independently, sign contracts, take out loans, start a business and get married—but still not legally allowed to buy alcohol. All of these factors militate against simple family rules that would ideally produce perfectly obedient children.

Our schools try hard. More than a decade ago a model drug education program was established at Bainbridge Island, Washington. It received considerable publicity and was touted as the wave of the future. The program ran for a dozen years and cost taxpayers millions of dollars. The schools involved were among the best in the state: the students tested well above the national average; the high school drop-out rate was extremely low; and approximately 80 percent went to college. On November 10, 1989, *The Wall Street Journal* featured an article about the program at Bainbridge Island entitled "Shunned Lessons: Even a School That Is a Leader in Drug War Grades Itself a Failure."

What happened? In 1977, Bainbridge Island schools developed an intensive drug education program starting in first grade and continuing through high school graduation. They included all the elements that were believed to be required for a first-rate drug education program: the writing of essays on drug problems, drug-refusal role-playing and exercises for building self-esteem and positive thinking. The result? A failure: approximately 70 percent of the students who participated in the program now use drugs or alcohol weekly, and 5 percent of the students in Bainbridge junior and senior high schools are chemically dependent. Yet because our government's "War on Drugs" places major emphasis on classroom education, many school systems are eagerly putting into place programs that are modeled after the Bainbridge effort—a program that failed to work! The superintendent of Bainbridge schools has expressed his doubts that any drug education program in this country can make a difference because "society is too big an opponent."

A Washington State University professor who studied the

Bainbridge program expressed disappointment with the lack of positive results and noted that our society is filled with messages about drugs and alcohol, ranging from tolerating drugs to glamorizing them, which conflict with drug education efforts. "In such an environment any effort to teach youngsters abstinence from such substances is a little like trying to promote chastity in a brothel." Students who had been part of the program called it "a joke" and noted that rebellion is a natural part of adolescence, so that one effect of years of emphasizing "Just Say No!" was to actually encourage them to "Just Say Yes."

A key factor missing in the Bainbridge program was parental involvement. In an effort to correct this, an anti-drug seminar was scheduled by an elementary school and drew only 40 out of 200 parents, such disinterest being typical in schools across the nation. Bainbridge Island's teachers, however, have not given up. Future efforts in their schools are designed to "wake up" parents with surveys about the actual extent of student drug and alcohol use. Of course, we hope they succeed. If they are not able to make it in a community such as theirs—affluent, highly educated and success-oriented—what chance do less fortunate areas in the United States have?

What steps should be taken at this point? Should awareness be increased? Make more funds available? California has spent a fortune on drug education. An administrator in the California Department of Education summed up their efforts by stating, "We've thrown $45 million over the last three years into drug education in our schools.... But as of yet, I don't think we can say what helps and what doesn't." The problem is not that alcohol education is starting too late; Bainbridge Island began to include students into their program shortly after kindergarten!

Why is it so tough to identify the problem with our drug education efforts? In 1976, two UCLA professors began a study that followed over 1500 junior high school students; the researchers recently concluded that "Focusing simply on handling peer pressure, such as the 'Just Say No' approaches, may placate concerned but naive parents, teachers and funding sources, but is an incomplete approach to confronting the task of preventing drug abuse."

In an alcohol-drenched society, it seems clear by now that

saying no to alcohol has very limited power to persuade. So what should be done? Harvard psychiatrist George Vaillant, author of the celebrated 20-year study, *The Natural History of Alcoholism: Causes, Patterns and Paths to Recovery* (1983), insists that if society is ever to deal effectively with alcohol, "one of the directions we should go is to teach children how to make intelligent drinking decisions." Joseph Matarazzo, a leading health psychologist and former President of the American Psychological Association, has called for health practitioners to begin helping those who drink socially to "learn to do so with less cost to themselves, to their families, their employers and to society."

The bottom line is that we as parents have to do more for our children. Expecting schools to handle it on their own is a cop-out (and it also has been proven ineffective). To rely on "talking to" kids with simple "No!" proclamations clearly doesn't work with the majority of teenagers. This approach has been—and still is— ineffective in affecting adolescent sexual behavior, clothing and hairstyles and just as ineffective when it comes to affecting drinking habits. As well, children often imitate the behaviors and habits that adults display.

What is needed now is a plan to *prevent* drinking problems to the best of our abilities. This will require a combination of methods: it must include *early intervention*; setting a good example of moderate drinking that your child can get used to from a very young age; talking with and teaching your child about the realities of the hazards of drinking and taking immediate action the minute there is the slightest suggestion that a problem with alcohol may be brewing.

Clearly, the common denominator of success is parental involvement. Our aim in this book is to offer a systematic method for parents to provide all the assistance that is necessary for their children to make an intelligent decision about whether to drink and, equally important, if they do decide to be drinkers, how much, how often and when they will drink. Parents will be urged to help their children explore honestly the pros and cons of drinking versus abstinence. We will provide the tools necessary for parents to help their children chose abstinence and maintain a sober lifestyle. An integral part of making this attempt successful

is teaching children how to handle the strong societal encouragement to drink. For those parents whose kids are already drinkers
(approximately 60 percent) we will be giving clear, step-by-step
guidelines and instructions for teaching their children how to use
alcohol responsibly—in other words, with the minimal amount of
risk to themselves, their friends, their families and society.

Parents usually tend to deal with the subjects of sex and
alcohol in similar ways when their children are involved. The lure
of sex is especially strong in today's society. To teens, sex seems
like an adventure, a mature activity and the mark of adulthood.
In addition, sex, like alcohol, is considered forbidden fruit for
youngsters, made especially alluring by the fact that it is an
activity supposedly reserved for older people. Most parents find
that the easiest approach to teenage sex is to avoid and ignore it,
despite the modern realization that openness between parents
and children is the best policy. Admittedly, it is easy to tell your
kids "No," look away from the many problems they are facing
and hope the problems will go away or that the kids will solve
them alone—but clearly this is unrealistic thinking. Surely most
teenagers have a substantial enough knowledge about sex to
know how to prevent unwanted pregnancies—and if they don't,
their parents certainly do—yet of all industrialized nations, the
United States has the highest unwanted pregnancy rate among
teenagers. Despite this fact (information most all parents are
surely aware of) we often see the same avoidance scenario among
parents when it comes to teens and alcohol. Like sex, alcohol
appeals to younger people because it is forbidden, because it
seems like such a "grown-up" thing to do, and we know that many
young people are often in a hurry to grow up. Also, because it is
so available and so flaunted, it is extremely hard for a youngster
to ignore.

It is time for parents to get involved and do more. But before
action can be taken, it is worthwhile to take a look at the positions
parents have typically taken in the past. Various versions of the
"No" approach are described below. Do any of them sound
familiar to you?

COMMON PARENTAL ROLES IN SAYING "NO"

Fear merchant

Dishing out large doses of fear and worry is a very common and usually ineffective way of dealing with the issue of teenage drinking. By portraying drinkers as mindless victims of "demon rum," as pathetic, burnt-out shells of uncontrolled consumption because they were ignorant and stupid enough to flirt with danger, will most likely cause today's youngsters to laugh. In the past, fear tactics were tried extensively with sex education, with driver's education and with drug education. All of these attempts were monumental failures. *Reefer Madness,* the anti-marijuana film made in the 1930s, was meant to instill the fear of God in its viewers with its warning of the alleged dangers of marijuana. It is now considered to be nothing short of ludicrous because of its overblown characterizations of the evils of marijuana. It is now available on video cassette as a historical comedy. Not only have fright tales failed as educational devices, they sometimes have the unfortunate effect of making young people believe that *nothing* the older generation says is likely to be true or reliable. Finally, fear campaigns based on distorted facts are a violation of honesty between people who care about each other. This can poison the relationship between adult and child, making a genuine partnership most unlikely. If you feel a need to try to motivate your kids by scaring them, at least scare them with facts, not with untruths. Far better is to avoid fear entirely.

Lecturer

Another popular parental "No" role is the "lecturer." There is great power in language, but this power diminishes quickly when words become lectures. Parents who think that they are attempting to "talk to" their children and "reason with them" often are really doing nothing more than lecturing them. Students have plenty of experience at school in ignoring adults who say things they find of little interest. Parents who imagine that "My child wouldn't dare tune me out" have probably forgotten their own childhood. Kids become expert at tuning out adults, and their favorite and most frequent target is the adult who delivers the lectures.

Warden

A home can at times become something like a prison where the parents serve as the resident wardens. Rules are made and enforced at the top, conduct is scrutinized, behavior is monitored, and absolute obedience to authority is demanded. Punishment is given when alleged violations occur; yet when children do things well and correctly, parents sometimes feel that they are just doing what children are supposed to do and therefore feel no need to give positive feedback. This "negative tracking" is not uncommon in work settings where the boss plays warden, in schools where the teacher plays warden and in sports where the coach plays warden. Typically this type of relationship, where there is a one-way flow of power, causes antagonism and inevitable resentment. Authority of this type may be necessary in a prison where a power relationship is mandated, but it is generally destructive in other situations. The parent who plays warden usually will drive a child to an eventual "prison break"—a move that may manifest itself as a lifelong escape from the parent and the loss of the chance of ever successfully establishing a meaningful relationship.

TYPICAL PARENTAL PITFALLS

Playing any of the above "No" roles exposes a parent to a number of pitfalls—bogs into which their energy can be put with no benefit to anyone. Try to take an objective look at yourself and your own behavior and see if you recognize many (or any) of the following cases. Have you been on the receiving end or perhaps even given any of the following a try?

"I am in charge here!"

Right, as a parent, you are in charge (as long as your child lives under your roof), but only to an extent; your role is *not* to be a warden or the boss. As well, the ability to control your children is limited by several considerations: the fact that you are frequently apart from your children and therefore cannot possibly monitor their behavior or discover disobedience at all times throughout the day; the multitude of choices children must—and do—make without being able to consult you (presuming they would ask you if you were there); and the duality of your role as the caring person who must provide both love and discipline if you are going to be a good and responsible parent.

The result of these conflicts is that most parents, not wanting to alienate their children, try to exercise at least a modicum of fairness, reasonableness and flexibility when it comes to exerting authority, thereby avoiding the risk of losing their child's affection. The parent who insists on being "in charge" in the way we have explained it will end up paying a very high price—and for what? Alienating their children? It's not worth it. In addition, because children will ultimately make the majority of their own decisions without consulting you anyway, you are at best only nominally "in charge." It may be true that you pay the bills, provide room and board and attempt to influence your children in positive ways, but you are not in charge of their behavior and the choices they make. The time will come when they are offered an alcoholic beverage and you are not there to assist them in their decision of whether or not to take it. However, if you have played your cards right, you will be able to have a significant influence on the decision they make, whether you are present or not. Indeed, a key aim in this book is to provide the tools parents need to positively affect the decisions their children will finally make. This can be accomplished by developing a relationship in which your child will want and seek your opinions because they trust your judgment and appreciate the way you respect and trust them.

"If I just love them enough, they'll be OK."

This comforting philosophy of parenting is something we call "The Blossom Theory." It assumes that if you shower children with enough love they will thrive and grow, much like a young sprouting plant that needs only water and fertilizer to reach its growth potential. But human beings are not seeds and do not just sprout and grow into healthy adults with nothing but a diet of endless love. Unlike plants, one of the main causes of maladaptive growth and undesirable behavior in children is misdirected parental love and attention. Some children who throw academy award temper tantrums often do so not because they feel unloved and want attention, but because they have been given overdoses of love and affection in response to the wrong behavior. Parents often indulge their children without realizing that doing so fosters a disregard for personal and social responsibilities, as well as a tendency toward being self-centered. When parents rely on love alone they fall victim to a kind of magical thinking, assuming that everything will be fine if they just give enough love. This kind of thinking allows parents to avoid dealing directly with troublesome issues like drinking. The only problem is that it seldom succeeds.

"Being a parent means doing what comes naturally."

If we were to ask a classroom full of young people, "How many of you think you would make a good mathematician?" a few hands might go up. If we asked, "How many would make a good professional tennis player?" a couple more raised hands might show. The same would be true if a class were asked about their expected success as a chemist, a fire fighter, senator or almost any vocation. But, interestingly, something very different happens if we ask, "How many of you think you would make a good parent?" Almost all of the children's hands would shoot up immediately. Children, like the rest of society, seem to assume that parenting, unlike nearly all other tasks in life, is a built-in part of human nature—an automatic, inherited and dependable trait. Yet when it comes to actually handling the responsibilities of being a parent, most people are woefully unprepared. Many parents express surprise that they are unable to deal with the very stressful job of being on duty 24 hours a day, not realizing that the stress and difficulties they experience are very normal.

The fact is that for human beings there are only a few simple things that are inborn and instinctual, such as an infant's sucking reflex. Most complex behavior patterns—like the skills involved in successful parenting—do not come naturally. Expecting parenting to be an automatic skill can sometimes cause parents to wonder if something is wrong with them because they don't seem to know instinctively how to do it. This can be an unsettling and disturbing experience that can lead to feelings of great inadequacy. Since those who feel this way often assume that everyone else is able to parent quite naturally, it is doubly difficult for them to ask for help—a situation that tends to ensure that their lack of parenting skills is unlikely to improve. Being a parent is a complicated job, with great rewards and sometimes great pain. Too bad it doesn't come naturally.

"Until you're 18, I'll be making your choices for you."

Ann Landers received the following disturbing letter from the worried parents of a teenage girl:*

> Dear Ann:
>
> My wife and I have been married 21 years and have a good marriage. Our problem is a 17-year-old daughter who became involved with drugs and alcohol four years ago.
>
> When Alice was 13 she was expelled from school. We got her into therapy but it didn't help. She was kicked out of three schools within 10 months.
>
> Two years ago Alice came home one night and assaulted her mother while I was at work. My wife was hospitalized for six weeks with a fractured skull.
>
> Right after that we moved to Michigan and bought a home with a full basement. As a form of punishment, we started to keep Alice in the basement for 24 hours when she broke her curfew, or if she came home high on drugs or alcohol.
>
> The 24-hour punishment somehow stretched into several months. Our daughter has been chained to her bed frame in our basement for three months now and we are afraid to let her out for fear of getting into trouble with the law. We know what we're doing is wrong, but we take care of our daughter's needs and at least we know where she is.

---

* Reprinted by courtesy of Ann Landers and Creators Syndicate.

Her attitude has become very hostile since she has been locked in the basement. When we serve her meals she curses us and throws things. The other day when I brought her upstairs for her once-a-week shower, she broke the bathroom window and cut her arm badly. We were able to stop the bleeding, but we are afraid that her arm is infected. The antibiotics we've been giving her don't seem to be working. We don't know how we can get her medical attention without arousing the suspicion of a doctor.

When Alice turns 18, we plan to release her from the basement and allow her to be on her own. Please ask God to forgive us and tell us what to do.

Needing Guidance in Detroit

Our readers will undoubtedly want to see what kind of advice Ann gave to these parents; her down-to-earth reply follows:

Dear Detroit:

You must do several things—in this order:

First: Unchain your daughter and take her to the emergency room of the nearest hospital at once. As things stand you are guilty of child abuse. If the girl doesn't get medical attention promptly you could be guilty of murder.

Second: Get a lawyer. You are going to need one.

Third: Consult a doctor as to what should be done about the girl. If she refuses to be treated for her drug and alcohol problem she must be hospitalized.

Your story is tragic. I feel terribly sorry for all of you.

As this shocking case so clearly illustrates, no one should be able to make choices for anyone else. The attempt to do so can produce a power struggle of major proportions. Many parents like to believe that they have the right to make choices for their children, but this is simply wishful thinking. To try to control a child's right of choice is to negate that child's individuality and to refuse to recognize that children are thinking, feeling beings. Some parents give the impression that they would like their children to be clones of themselves—with identical values, ideals and beliefs to theirs. But children are persons who think, act and ultimately make decisions on their own, often regardless of the punishments they receive for exerting their individuality.

"It is faster and easier to do it myself."

One of the primary ways children learn to be irresponsible is when their parents deny them the opportunity to try and do things by themselves, although failure may be inevitable. Parents may become impatient with the time it takes children to do even simple tasks, and say, "Here, let me do it for you." What message do children get from this type of attitude? That slow, incompetent work, procrastination and dawdling, fooling around and side-stepping assigned tasks all pay off; someone else will inevitably do the job for them. When parents do this, their children can become lazy, shiftless and irresponsible. And why shouldn't kids take advantage of this solution to problems; irresponsibility seems so easy and works just fine in their family. When these children become adults they will most likely maintain this bad habit, doing what they know best.

"My child must be rescued."

Some parents complain of the burden of repeatedly having to rescue their kids. "Poor thing, just can't get along without me! I have to bail him out, pay his fine, make his excuses and get him off the hook, no matter what." The parent who acts as the all-too-ready rescuer is likely to produce children who, when they get in trouble, are quite willing to give all of their personal control and decisions to others. Because they have always been "rescued" in the past they have little concept of the meaning of personal responsibility and have never been required to take care of themselves. Since others usually bear the consequences of their behavior, they have little incentive to learn from mistakes or develop mature and effective ways of handling life's problems.

Strategies of avoidance

All of the above approaches to the parent-child relationship are variations on the "No" approach: "No, you cannot have any input in family decisions because I am in charge"; "No, my children don't need guidelines, they just need lots of love"; "No, I don't need to worry about learning how to be a good parent. I'll just do what comes naturally"; "No point in concerning yourself with questions about drinking, young lady, since I'll be making those decisions until you are 18"; "No problem, you are safe from the natural consequences of your actions because I'll always be here to rescue you. " Each of these are strategies of avoidance, usually used unwittingly by well-intentioned parents. We can do better.

AN ALTERNATIVE APPROACH

Until their children reach the age of 5 or so, parents almost constantly have to monitor their behavior to ensure their safety and well-being. Responsible parents will influence what kids do by actual physical control if necessary until their children develop some self-protective skills and a degree of self-sufficiency. Between the ages of 5 and 9, the relationship becomes increasingly verbal and parents are able to discipline their kids by setting limits and making rules, allowing them to enjoy the good things of life while at the same time exerting fair and reasonable discipline. Above age 9, the wise parent more actively shapes independence and helps the child move toward making his or her own decisions as well as living with the consequences of those decisions, even when they are unpleasant. It is indeed possible to assume the dual parental role of teacher and fair disciplinarian as opposed to the "warden." Children are not seen as clones, but as growing individuals, in transition, in passage, going somewhere with eyes toward a future of their own choice. This facilitator relationship fosters positive interaction between parent and child, with mutual warmth and respect that should last a lifetime.

Step 3 will explore the process of developing a facilitating and influential relationship, particularly as it relates to drinking. But before parents or teens can deal rationally with the subject of alcohol, the basic facts must be known.

Step 2

Getting the Facts about Alcohol

Whether you drink or not, knowing the facts about alcohol will give you a significant advantage when dealing with drinking issues. Virtually every culture in human history has discovered some means of pleasantly altering the state of consciousness either by smoking, drinking, sniffing or eating a particular substance. Even some animals seem to enjoy chewing plants or fruits that produce an altered state. Noted psychopharmacologist Ron Siegal has suggested that experiencing an altered state of consciousness may be a natural drive common to all higher animals.

Why do people drink? The reason is not at all surprising—it feels good and it tastes good. Most people usually have to acquire a taste for the flavor of alcohol, but once they do, the taste of the drink adds to the pleasurable effects of alcohol. There are, of course, many experiences that are enjoyable to people, such as sex, music and roller coaster rides, just to name a few. That pleasure alone is a sufficient motivation to pursue an activity is easily understandable. When children ask adults why people drink, it is dishonest—not to mention unnecessary—to invent reasons that are untrue. Not only can children handle the truth, they prefer it.

Whether you are a drinker or not, it makes sense to understand the basic facts about alcohol. Whoever you are and whatever kind of lifestyle you live, alcohol is certain to have some impact on your life; so it makes sense to be educated about it.

BLOOD ALCOHOL

Let's consider alcohol, first from a medical point of view. What actually occurs when alcohol enters the stomach? How does alcohol affect a person's brain and behavior? Are there ways to alter its effects, to predict how strong these effects will be, and are there methods to prevent excessive use? All of these questions (and others) hinge on an understanding of blood alcohol level (commonly referred to as BAL or simply BA). Understanding blood alcohol is an essential part of understanding the effects of drinking, just as understanding the role of calories is essential to learning about weight loss and gain.

Blood alcohol level refers to the percentage of alcohol in the bloodstream. In other words, your body contains a certain volume of blood (about 5 quarts) and when you drink alcoholic beverages the alcohol goes from the stomach to the bloodstream. The body burns the alcohol off or "metabolizes" it. The relative amount of alcohol in the blood can be expressed in terms of a percentage; if you weigh approximately 150 pounds and consume four or five drinks in 1 hour, the percentage of alcohol in your blood will usually be over one-tenth of 1 percent (or one-thousandth of your total blood volume). This figure, 0.10 percent blood alcohol, is the cut-off point for being legally intoxicated in many states (although there is currently a movement toward lowering the legal BA level). Of course, the larger a person is, the greater the blood volume, so if you weigh more, you have to drink more alcohol than a smaller person would to have the same percentage of alcohol in your body.

Because of two factors, your blood volume and the time your body takes to burn off alcohol, the alcohol level is closely tied to your *weight* and the *speed* of your drinking. To determine an accurate BA for yourself or someone else (without the aid of a device that does it electrochemically), you need to know how much the person weighs, the number of drinks consumed and the length of time spent drinking. With this information and a simple BA chart based on weight (found at the back of this book), you can quickly arrive at the BA. The BA is a reliable measure of how high one is from drinking, whether or not one is legally drunk, as well as being a dependable way of assessing whether one drinks too much.

An alternative (and more exact) method for determining the blood alcohol level employs a BA device like those used with drunk driving suspects. (Police prefer breathalizers because they are simple to use, but such devices have no way of determining how much or for how long a suspect has been drinking.) All a breathalizer requires is a simple blow into a tube and the device will calculate the amount of alcohol in a person's breath, an indirect but accurate measure of how much alcohol is in the blood. Some states allow drunk-driving suspects to choose other methods of BA calculation, such as blood or urine tests.

The approaches described above measure the same thing and will give the same accurate results when conducted properly. It is possible to purchase a personal breath analysis device. Some of the less expensive ones depict a simple traffic-signal green/amber/red light indicating safe/borderline/drunk levels of intoxication; a more costly model displays three-digit BA readings. Personal breath testers range in price from under $100 to over $400 for a court-acceptable, hand-held model. These devices can be particularly useful in helping drinkers assess whether or not they should drive a motor vehicle (see Intoximeters in the references at the end of the book).

The night before beginning work on this particular chapter, one of the authors attended a wedding reception where fine champagne flowed freely. A couple of friends appeared to be consuming extremely generous amounts, so as they were discussing driving home, someone suggested that each of them breathe into a BA device. The husband registered a BA of 0.148, far above the legally drunk cutoff figure of 0.08 used in California. His wife, on the other hand, showed a readout of 0.053, suggesting that she too was impaired by her drinking, but at least she was not legally drunk nor was she as likely to drive as dangerously as her husband. That precipitated another discussion of whether they should call a cab, or, if not, who should drive home. This brief breath test may very possibly have saved someone's life that night.

The usual method of presenting BA figures in terms of decimals tends to be awkward, so for convenience throughout the rest of this book we will simply eliminate the decimal by multi-plying each numeral by 1000 (or, moving the decimal three points to the right). Thus, a BA of 0.100 becomes 100 and a BA of 0.050 becomes 50. It is easy with this decimal-free system to think of BAs as being like miles per hour with zero indicating standing still, 100 like driving 100 miles per hour (a very high and dangerous figure) and 55 the legal speed limit. Clearly, if 55 mph is considered a safe speed limit and you are driving at 100 mph, you are taking a big risk. There are actually several good reasons to think of 55 as a reasonable BA limit: when drinkers go beyond this level, they tend to feel drunker, but not necessarily better. Emotional control and coordination deteriorate, hangovers are more likely, and abusive drinking patterns become more frequent.

What happens when blood alcohol levels rise?

To see what happens to our experience and behavior with increas-ing levels of blood alcohol, consider the following chart:

BA Level	Behavioral Effects
25	Warm; pleasant; mellow; less inhibited
55	Relaxed; less alert; feels "a buzz"; driving somewhat impaired
75	Feels high; floating; may respond to situations with exaggerated emotion; coordination worse
100	Uninhibited; often noisy; embarrassing; talkative; obnoxious; driving very impaired
150	Obviously intoxicated; inability to think sensibly; trouble walking, talking and driving
300	Falling-down drunk
500	Loss of consciousness; risk of death

Exactly why does alcohol affect a person in these ways? Essentially because alcohol depresses (slows down) brain cells; the higher the BA the larger the portion of your brain that is put out of action. The human brain is an engineering marvel in which tens of billions of individual cells work together in complex harmony and in a delicate chemical balance. Alcohol alters that balance and disrupts the organization in the brain, which is the center for everything that happens to both mind and body. When brain function is disrupted—and the intake of alcohol is just one of many ways that this can happen—we may have trouble receiving and processing information, thinking rationally and carrying out even the simplest of acts. Various chemical analyses have attempted to explain how alcohol changes brain activity: one such explanation maintains that alcohol interferes with the brain's access to oxygen; another claims that alcohol alters the chemistry of nerve fibers in the brain, thus changing their ability to transmit electrochemical impulses to the rest of the body. We know that *heavy* consumption of alcohol will eventually damage brain cells, enough to accumulate over a period of years and produce some commonly observed brain disorders long known to be linked to alcohol use. One tragic aspect of the town drunk is the realization that because he has been drinking long enough and heavy enough, there is no possibility of regaining fully normal brain function. The brain is permanently damaged and only limited improvement can ever be expected, even with abstinence.

What determines your blood alcohol?

Alcohol travels to the brain through the bloodstream after being absorbed by the stomach walls and small intestine. (Alcohol is one of the few substances absorbed by the stomach; most others are absorbed by the intestine several hours after eating. This explains the prompt effect of alcohol after drinking beer, wine or hard liquor.) How fast alcohol is absorbed and how high your BA rises depends in part on what is in your stomach, what you drink and the manner in which you drink; if you gulp straight whiskey you will get drunk faster than if you slowly sip a tall whiskey and soda. Consuming drinks that contain a lot of mixer, drinking slowly and combining your drinking with eating (or already having a full stomach) will cause a slower increase in BA and a lower peak BA (the highest level of alcohol reached). Also, alcoholic drinks that are combined with mixers containing sugar, fats or milk tend to slow down the body's absorption of alcohol and therefore will keep the peak BA level down. If you have recently eaten a big meal and then have a couple of drinks, it will take twice as long to reach the peak BA as it would if you had an empty stomach. So, eating while drinking is a good idea because it slows down the effects of alcohol. But, if you drink enough, no amount of food will hold back the inevitable...you will get drunk.

ALCOHOL AS A DEPRESSANT

Alcohol is often described as a "depressant." This can be confusing because the word depressant would seem to mean something that causes depression, but this is not quite the case. In fact, many drinkers get lightheaded and playful when they drink—hardly the behavior of a depressed person.

A depressant is something that decreases the function or activity of the body, not the depression of a person's mood. In large quantities alcohol acts something like a general anesthetic, such as ether. The depressant effect begins by reducing the activity of the higher brain centers such as those that control vision, thought, speech and movement. This process also diminishes control over behavior and emotions, which is why drinkers tend to behave impulsively and are over-emotional at times. With increasing BA levels, alcohol begins to slow the deeper and more primitive brain centers that regulate vital bodily functions such as heart rate, breathing and sleeping. In other words, it is not one's mood that is depressed by alcohol, but the functioning of the brain. This is why it is risky to mix alcohol and prescription drugs such as sleeping pills, because both depress brain function and when taken together they work in a cumulative manner. In fact, the combination of alcohol and pills can so severely depress the functioning of the brain that respiration or the heartbeat may cease, and with it, life.

You cannot counteract the effects of alcohol or speed up the rate of metabolism once alcohol is in the system. A common bit of misinformation, dangerous because it is incorrect, is that coffee can reduce the effects of alcohol and help sober up a drunk person. In fact, nothing has yet been discovered that will effectively make a drinker's brain function more normally in terms of perception, reaction time or judgment. Caffeine may briefly make a drunk person feel more alert, but this too can cause an unexpected problem: because of a temporary sense of feeling less drunk, a person might be more willing to put himself behind the wheel of a car. The erroneous belief that a reduction in sleepiness means greater sobriety has probably been responsible for many driving deaths. There is no magic path to achieve instant sobriety after alcohol is already in the blood. You cannot jog to "burn it off," urinating will not "drain it out," gobbling a sandwich will not "soak it up," drinking coffee will not "take off the edge," nor can you make yourself sober by hard concentration, meditation or positive thinking.

DRINK EQUIVALENTS

In order to estimate your BA at any time, you first have to determine how much alcohol you have consumed. Count how many standard drinks you've had and whether you've been drinking wine, beer or mixed drinks. Each bottle has its own label and will state either the percentage of alcohol or the proof. Proof is easily converted to percentage by simply dividing it in half, so any liquor that is 80 proof will be 40 percent alcohol. (Most vodkas, whiskeys and gins are 80 or 86 proof.)

The typical alcohol content of several popular beverages is shown below:

Beverage	Percent Alcohol
Hard liquor (bourbon, vodka, gin)	40
Liqueurs (crème de menthe, Benedictine)	28
Sweet wines (sherry, port, muscatel)	20
Dry wines (Chenin blanc, Burgundy, Chablis)	12
Malt beverages (stout, porter)	6-7
Ale	5-6
Beer	4-5

Of course, this does not mean that there are no exceptions. Vodka and rum, while generally available in both 80 and 100 proof (40 and 50 percent alcohol), also come in even higher proof, and the alcohol content of different wines and malt beverages may vary depending upon production methods. But on the whole, the depending upon production methods. But on the whole, the guidelines listed above allow for comparison of the amount of alcohol consumed and facilitate calculating approximate drink equivalents.

Most shot glasses contain 1 to 1 1/2 ounces of alcohol; therefore, we will use the average of 1 1/4 ounces for our standard drink of hard liquor and make the following comparisons:

one shot of hard liquor (1 1/4 oz.) =
one small glass of sweet wine (2 1/2 oz.) =
one medium glass of dry wine (4 oz.) =
one large glass of beer (12 oz.).

These drinks are nearly equivalent in terms of alcohol content since 1.25 oz. of a beverage that is 40 percent alcohol (such as whiskey) gives 0.5 oz. of *pure* alcohol (1.25 times 0.40), and 12 oz. of a beverage that is on average 4.5 percent alcohol (such as beer) gives 0.54 oz. of pure alcohol (12 times 0.045). It sometimes takes a minute to accept the fact that drinking one beer and drinking one mixed drink means taking equal (equivalent) amounts of alcohol—actually, beer is slightly more. We have had people tell us, "Oh, I don't drink much, just beer...maybe a sixpack on a weekend day, sometimes a twelvepack." With a little calculating you will discover that these self-described "light drinkers" ("just beer") will actually have consumed more alcohol than that contained in half a bottle of vodka or whiskey. Twelve beers are the equivalent of about 16 oz. of 80-proof whiskey (a fifth of whiskey contains 25.6 oz.).

It should be apparent that if you are to keep accurate track of your alcohol consumption you must pay close attention to how much and what you are drinking, just as a dieter must carefully record what he or she eats in order to count calories. So remember, without counting the number of drinks you've had, it is impossible for you to accurately estimate your blood alcohol level.

Say you went to a dinner party and had two mixed drinks before dinner and then two glasses of wine during dinner, a total of four drinks. If you then added a couple of glasses of beer (you might guess they were about 8 oz. each), that would be a little over one more drink to add to your total alcohol intake.

Part of the problem of trying to be attentive to how much and how fast you are drinking is that not everyone plays with the same rules. If someone else is making your drinks and you are drinking mixed drinks, make sure to watch while they are being made and request that the bartender use only one shot per drink—and from a *regular* shot glass, not a giant "Texas shot glass." Also, be alert to the host or hostess who uses the "approximately half an inch in the glass" method of mixing hard-liquor drinks. At a party a few years ago, the authors gave a BA test to a woman who seemed too intoxicated to drive home. Her breath lit up the red (danger) light on the breathalizer, indicating a BA of over 100. She was astonished to discover this: "I can't be drunk, I've only had two gin and tonics." She was right in thinking that she could not have achieved such an elevated BA level after having only two drinks, especially in light of the fact that she was not exactly slender. We asked to see the glass she had used and tell us how her drinks had been mixed. She went to the sink and retrieved a French storage jar that measured about four inches wide and five inches high. She put in a few cubes of ice, filled the glass halfway with gin and then topped it of with tonic. We calculated that each of her "only two drinks" actually contained about five shots of gin. Prudently, she decided to ride home with someone else.

Some people might feel that they are doing their guests a favor or perhaps are being attentive hosts by conscientiously keeping everyone's glasses full. When people do this, it makes it impossible to know how many drinks you've had. It is not bad manners to request normal-strength drinks and to inform your host that you are counting your drinks (or your calories) and that you must keep careful track of your alcohol intake.

It is difficult to try to record the number of drinks you've had when drinking beer, wine or margaritas from a pitcher. Studies have shown that college students will drink considerably more beer when it is served in a pitcher than when they drink it from a bottle and they will also consistently underestimate how much they have had when they are drinking in this manner. When drinking from a pitcher or a keg it is easy to misjudge the number a person must confront the visible evidence of empty bottles in front of him, he cannot deny or miscalculate the number of drinks consumed (and for this reason, it is a good idea to ask the server in a bar or restaurant to leave the empties).

CALCULATING YOUR BLOOD ALCOHOL LEVEL

If you keep count of the number of drinks you've had, know your approximate weight and keep track of the length of time you've been drinking (at one sitting), you can determine your BA easily. For example, let's say you are a 140-pound female. You've spent two hours at a party and have consumed a total of four drinks. By looking at the table below (also shown in more detail in the back of the book), you can figure out what your blood alcohol level would be:

Number of Hours Spent Drinking

Number of Drinks	1	2	3	4	5	6	7
1	15	0	0	0	0	0	0
2	50	30	15	0	0	0	0
3	80	65	50	30	15	0	0
4	115	95	80	65	50	35	15
5	145	130	115	95	80	65	50
6	175	160	145	130	115	95	80
7	210	195	175	160	145	130	115
8	240	225	210	195	175	160	145
9	275	255	240	225	210	195	175
10	305	290	275	255	240	225	210

As you can see, only on the basis of number of drinks consumed and length of drinking, your blood alcohol would be a dangerously high 95, making you legally drunk in many states. Had you consumed only two drinks, your BA would be 30—under the moderate limit of 55, but still significantly high and at a level that would impair your ability to drive safely. By checking the full table in the back of this book for a 180-pound male, you will see that if he had consumed the same number of drinks (four) in the table in the back of this book for a 180-pound male, you will see that if he had consumed the same number of drinks (four) in the same period of time (two hours), his BA would be only 50. However, if a 100-pound woman drank four drinks in two hours, she would be staggering drunk with a BA of 150. If the 180-pound man and the 100-pound woman were attending a social function together and they each drank four drinks in two hours, her BA would be three times as high as his! It is rare for couples to weigh the same, but it is not uncommon for them to match each other drink for drink. Understandably, this is a highly dangerous practice.

Most of you know how much you weigh and, therefore, it is a relatively minor task to sit down and spend a few minutes studying the weight charts in the back of this book so that you can memorize how high you will be in one hour after having had one, two, three or four drinks. With this information, you will know when it is necessary to avoid drinking too much.

Note that in these weight charts the BAs for women are higher than those given for men who are the same weight. Recent research suggests that men produce more of a certain enzyme than women do, and this enzyme begins the rapid absorption of alcohol in the stomach. More alcohol will therefore get into a woman's bloodstream, making her BA higher than a man who weighs the same and has had the same number of drinks.

Other factors may interact with your BA: how tired you are, whether your body is in shape and whether you are on medications, just to name a few. Each of these can change the way alcohol affects you.

THE EFFECTS OF ALCOHOL ON HEALTH

The health risks associated with heavy drinking are well known and have been highly publicized. The greatest media attention is given to the most dramatic—drunk driving, but suicide and domestic violence, which are equally dramatic, are also frequently caused by drinking. As well, drunken behavior is considered to be a major cause of accidental falls and burns. Impulsive behavior is very common after drinking and plays a major role in many accidents. For example, after several drinks, an acquaintance of the authors decided to repair a TV antenna. He climbed onto the roof and proceeded to fall off. He staggered into the house and was found dead on the bathroom floor later that evening. He was not yet 40 years old.

Recent concern about fetal alcohol syndrome (FAS) has prompted the government to require warnings on alcoholic beverage containers and also in public places that serve alcohol. In a nutshell, FAS can occur when pregnant women take even moderate amounts of alcohol and may result in a variety of physical or developmental abnormalities in their children. Some speculate that if a pregnant woman drinks, she is taking the risk of causing behavioral problems in the child that may not be accompanied by any obvious physical abnormality at birth. A woman who goes on a one-night drinking binge while pregnant may cause a chemical assault on the developmental processes occurring in her fetus at that moment. For example, if facial formation is at a stage of rapid progression, it may be altered, producing odd features as the main sign of FAS. If higher brain development is at a critical point, the brain may fail to develop properly and with it the capacity to learn from experience. This could explain lifelong behavioral difficulties. A woman who drinks constantly during pregnancy naturally incurs greater risk and the more she drinks at each sitting, the greater the risk. Since nobody knows the quantity of various chemicals required to negatively influence a growing fetus, it makes sense to avoid all chemical risks including alcohol, nicotine and caffeine.

Drinking alcohol also places the liver at risk. Normally, it does 80 to 90 percent of the work of metabolizing alcohol, removing the equivalent of about one drink per hour from the body. Alcohol causes a gradual buildup of fatty deposits in the liver, making it less efficient at eliminating many waste products, including alcohol. With sufficient damage, eventual liver failure will occur and the body becomes unable to detoxify undesirable products, resulting in coma and a most unpleasant death. Cirrhosis of the liver was once thought to be caused by the poor eating habits common to heavy drinkers, but it is now believed that alcohol has a direct and toxic effect on the liver, even with an acceptable diet. Early alcohol-related liver problems can be improved if drinking is stopped, but cirrhosis is incurable except by liver transplant, which has been found to be successful, but very expensive. The actual rate of cirrhosis has been declining steadily in the U.S. since 1973, and nobody is sure exactly why, but nevertheless it remains a serious public health problem, being the ninth leading cause of death in America.

Alcoholic beverages have a very high number of calories compared to other drinks, and calories for many of us mean unwanted pounds. Those excess pounds strain various organ systems and lead to diabetes and high blood pressure, among other diseases. There are no proteins, vitamins or minerals in the calories derived from alcohol; however, heavy drinkers often experience a loss of appetite, so their overall nutrition suffers, adding a further health risk. We also know that heavy alcohol consumption over a period of time reduces the resiliency of the immune system. Also it decreases the body's ability to absorb various amino acids, vitamins and sugars needed for good health, possibly by damaging the lining of the intestines. Drinking can adversely affect blood pressure, aggravate hypertension and directly reduce the strength and pumping ability of the heart muscle. It doesn't take much imagination to picture the long-term combination of these negative health factors and to understand why moderation, as in most things, is especially important for drinkers.

It is interesting to note that despite the obvious health hazards associated with heavy drinking, some research suggests that *light* drinkers are actually healthier in some respects than nondrinkers. The claim is that a little bit of alcohol may be beneficial to one's general health and longevity (perhaps by its ability to lower cholesterol) but alcohol researchers and educators are reluctant to mention these possible benefits for fear that it would backfire providing drinkers with an excuse to drink excessively ("If one drink is good for me, think what great shape I'll be in after four drinks!") or encourage daily drinking that can lead to tolerance and escalating consumption. It is ironic, as was recently pointed out by a Napa Valley, California winemaker, that the government now requires warnings on wine bottles about the danger of abuse, but prohibits any mention of studies that suggest moderate drinking might be healthful. Publications such as *The Moderation Journal* and Gene Ford's book, *The Benefits of Moderate Drinking*, imply that the government is proceeding on a track of "neo-prohibition" and becoming "anti-alcohol." Ford believes that some national policymakers are attempting to lump alcohol use together with illicit drug-taking, raising the cost of liquor and reducing its availability with the assumption that zero consumption is the best way to national health. Indeed, a former director of the National Institute on Alcohol Abuse and Alcoholism (NIAAA) has been quoted as stating that, "Alcohol is the dirtiest drug we have. It permeates and damages all tissue. No other drug can cause the same degree of harm as it does." Some express concern that such extreme positions have influenced government policy and politics, producing a clear shift from a position of being anti-abuse to a harder line of being anti-*use* (shades of Prohibition). The most rational approach, we believe, is to be either a nondrinker or a light drinker and under those conditions your health will not be seriously affected by alcohol.

A discussion of alcohol and health and illness cannot conclude without mentioning a few words about hangovers. Nobody ever died from one, but some hangover sufferers surely have wished they had: the agony of a throbbing headache, dry mouth, upset stomach, inability to concentrate and irritability can often be simply unbearable—and there is no cure except time. Aspirin may help a bit, and while many tout various "miracle cures," none of them does any real good. Having another drink ("hair of the dog that bit you") certainly does not work; at best it may give a few minutes of relief, but it only prolongs the ability of your body to return to normal. The recovery process may take 24 hours and usually that block of time is a dead loss since few of us are able to do efficient or productive work when suffering from a hangover. The misery experienced during a bad hangover is well illustrated by the literal translation of the slang terms used for it in various languages: the Germans call it "Katzenjammer," which means "wailing of cats"; to the French it is "La Gueule de Bois," or "woody mouth"; Norwegians suffer "Jeg Har Tommermen," or "workmen in my head"; Swedes have "Hont I Haret," or "pain in the roots of my hair"; Italians experience "Stonato," or being "out of tune"; and the Spanish experience "Resaca," the "surf of the sea." Even though the heavy-drinking Russians may swear by salted cucumber juice as the best hangover treatment and the Norwegians drink a glass of heavy cream, the only real way to affect a hangover is to prevent it by watching how much you drink, keeping your BA below 55 and avoiding dark-colored drinks with strong aromas, which contain more "congeners" (impurities) than light-colored drinks (congeners seem to contribute to the degree of hangover experienced).

ALCOHOL AND SEX

Drinking alcohol lowers one's inhibitions, so while under the influence, many people have an easier time engaging in certain activities that they might normally be more reserved about. A good example: when people drink they often engage in romantic activities and sex with more abandon than usual. Since teens (as well as adults) often have distorted notions about the effects of alcohol on sexual performance, a comment on this subject is pertinent. Although it is true that even a little bit of alcohol can lower your inhibitions and make you feel more amorous, a large amount will generally interfere with your sexual abilities by reducing sensitivity and reflexes, such as achieving and maintaining an erection. In *Macbeth*, Shakespeare correctly observed that alcohol "provokes the desire, but it takes away the performance." In addition, when you are drinking and trying to have an intimate relationship, the decrease in your awareness of nuances in verbal and nonverbal behavior may actually turn a person off, resulting in rejection rather than romance. If you end up getting drunk, your chances of amour will be seriously diminished since few people can tolerate a drunken lover. A more serious matter is that when teenagers get drunk, their judgment becomes diminished and they tend to act impulsively, engaging in sex that can—and often does—result in unwanted pregnancies. Sexually transmitted diseases as a consequence of drinking deserve mention. Clearly, a person with an impaired frame of mind may not be as careful about avoiding sexually dangerous situations, such as not using protection or having spur-of-the-moment sex with someone they don't know. This problem has intensified greatly with the current AIDS epidemic.

TOLERANCE TO ALCOHOL

Developing a tolerance is a topic of primary importance in understanding alcohol abuse (see Step 7), since it is a potential hazard for everyone who drinks. "Short-term tolerance" means that in a single drinking episode, a drinker adapts to the effects of alcohol. This can be likened to the experience of entering an Italian restaurant; the initial strong and striking smell of garlic fades away in a short time. The odor is still there, but you just no longer notice it. This same kind of adaption occurs every time you drink. You may feel quite a buzz at a BA of 30 during the second of three drinks, but feel almost nothing at all a couple of hours later when your declining BA falls to the same level of 30. "Long-term tolerance" means that regular, and particularly heavier drinkers do not feel as high after consuming the same amount of alcohol as they used to in their early days of drinking. If you drink every day, developing some long-term tolerance is almost inevitable. After a period of time, because two drinks no longer provide the high they once did, you may now have to consume three drinks to get the same effect that two drinks used to produce. After a while, when three doesn't seem to do it, you can move up to four drinks. People who drink large quantities of alcohol daily may drink to a BA of legal intoxication and report feeling almost nothing. This does not, however, mean that they are sober; it means they have been abusing alcohol. Their BA will be exactly where expected, their coordination is influenced as negatively as expected (although perhaps not as much as with a lighter drinker) and their judgment will be impaired. They just do not feel high, so to get the pleasant buzz they want they must drink more and more. They become poor judges of how high they actually are. It used to be thought that long-term tolerance took years to develop and this is still considered an important sign of alcohol dependence. Yet in one of our own experiments we found that within a *week* of increasing the daily alcohol consumption of light drinkers (volunteers who did not drink daily and normally drank to a BA under 35), a significant increase in tolerance occurred. In addition to a direct measure of tolerance, we found that in a party situation where subjects were told to drink as much as they wished in order to feel as high as they usually do, these drinkers unwittingly consumed nearly twice as much alcohol as they did before the experiment. The tolerance these normal drinkers acquired was reversed within a week of abstinence. This research suggests that without realizing it *all* drinkers run the risk of increasing their tolerance to alcohol and becoming abusers.

The best way to deal with the risk of tolerance is simply not to drink daily—just drink occasionally. Save alcohol for special events, rather than making it part of your daily routine. Perhaps the most important fact for drinkers to realize about alcohol is that what feels best is a *rising* blood alcohol starting from a zero level in a person who is not tolerant to alcohol. You feel a warm buzz that is best during the first drink or two when your BA goes up. You will not feel better at higher BAs, so it is wise to quit before the red-light 55 BA is reached. A comprehensive list of sensible drinking guidelines is given when we get to Step 6.

We conclude by noting that beginning drinkers, which means most teen drinkers, have no tolerance to the effects of alcohol and no experience in controlling the amount they drink. Drinkers usually learn how much is too much by trial and error. In addition to having no tolerance or experience, teenagers often have smaller bodies (and thus higher BAs from the same amount of alcohol as heavier people), poorer judgment and less practice in self-control. Also, since teenagers have more energy and higher activity levels, the disinhibiting effects of alcohol may result in more impulsive and dangerous behavior. For these reasons, teenage drinkers are at greater risk than adults.

Step 3

Maximizing Parental Influence

A CASE STUDY

Seeing the world through the eyes of a 15-year-old is very different from seeing the world from an adult perspective. Matthew is a typical example. He feels vaguely inadequate, is somewhat distressed about his looks and wishes that others liked him and were more accepting. He has practically no idea of how others really see him and he is not sure who he really is. He tries out various roles such as clown and nice guy, but feels he isn't very good at anything, although most others regard him as a pleasant young man and a reasonably good student and athlete. He wants very much for girls to like him and be attracted to him, and he experiences strong sexual feelings, as do most adolescent boys. Matt loves and wants to please his parents and has a positive though somewhat superficial relationship with them. They are not attuned to his personal concerns and problems, which he himself has difficulty understanding or discussing with anyone. His parents do express their interest in his life and advise him on their availability for discussion of any problems he may have, but like most youngsters, he rarely turns to them for assistance with any problems. Matt has no "claim to fame," he is not a leader, nor does he stand out in sports, academics or in the social world of high school. In addition, Matt has no real feel for what it means to be his own person. Because of this inability he has no practice in standing up to his peers' persuasions, and he doesn't want to risk alienating them by doing so.

Some of the things Matt wants in life are: acceptance by other kids; greater independence; to feel like a "man"—an adult; to have a girlfriend; to express his adventurous urges; and to feel good about himself, which means experiencing less self-doubt and anxiety.

One night Matt finds himself with some friends who have a twelvepack of beer. Everyone is drinking except him, so he feels uncomfortable and different. He knows he is not supposed to drink at all (according to predetermined family rules) and says "no" several times. He thinks about how he often sees others drink beer without any problem and at that moment it looks like it would be fun and not really dangerous. He decides to just go ahead and see if he can get away with it; no one except his friends need ever know. He drinks one beer and it feels very good. In an altered state of mild euphoria and diminished judgment, he succumbs fairly easily to pressure from his peers to have a second and then a third beer. Having never drunk before, he becomes high rapidly, doesn't feel very good, but is enormously reinforced by the admiration of his buddies for being "macho." He also discovers that this feeling of being high makes him no longer concerned about his looks or what people think about him—a pleasant relief. So he downs a fourth beer. This is how a perfectly nice young man like Matt—a previous nondrinker—might come home drunk, to the distress of his parents.

Could Matt's parents have done more? The answer is yes. Could they have done something to prevent this from happening in the first place? Again, the answer is yes. Finally, what should they do now that this has happened?

This step will provide you with specific strategies of parenting that will help you to handle various situations. Using even *some* of the strategies should improve the quality of the relationship you have with your children and give you greater influence on their behavior and overall development (for more detailed suggestions see *Surviving with Kids* by Bartz and Rasor). Although these strategies apply to raising children in general, here we will tailor them to concerns about teens and drinking alcohol. Any developing issue—drugs, sex, independence, drinking—is best approached by establishing an open and trusting relationship with your child, one that allows parents access to the child's world. Our purpose here is to help parents lay the foundation for a mutually satisfying, life-long relationship that will make them a reliable and helpful resource to their children. Their children will be able to come to them with questions about alcohol and sex as well as other problems and concerns (I got drunk last night; I'm failing algebra; I had a big fight with my best friend last night; I'm pregnant).

Children are not small adults. They are unique individuals who perceive themselves and others in ways that differ greatly from the ways adults see things (a point we mean to keep stressing). Kids behave according to how *they* see things, not in the way adults tell them to behave. As children develop, different issues and conflicts arise. Judgment calls, decision-making and responsibility are especially important abilities that improve as children mature and these are precisely the areas in which parents and concerned others can exert positive influence. How to maximize this influence is the main goal of this chapter. The younger your kids are, the better because they are still developing and do not yet have inflexible ideas already forged in their minds. If they are older or are already having problems with alcohol, these principles and techniques will enable you to deal with those problems more effectively.

General characteristics of the ideal parent include (1) to be trustworthy, reliable and consistent; (2) to have control of their own emotions so they will respond to *their children's behavior*, not react *according to the mood they happen to be in at the time*; (3) to tolerate mistakes; (4) to be available to their children (and not just for "quality time"); (5) to know where their kids are and what they are doing; (6) to listen well; (7) to try to help their children understand themselves and others better; and (8) to be able to appropriately, not destructively, discipline their children. Above all, while avoiding overindulgence, it is essential for parents to provide a loving and caring atmosphere, even when there are aspects of their children's behavior that they don't care for.

Admittedly, this is a rather intimidating list, but it is easier to cultivate some of these ideal parental characteristics if you know what it is you're striving toward. You will also be on the right track if you understand that what most children want is entirely normal. It is how they go about meeting their needs and wants that can be upsetting and unacceptable to parents. *Helping your children learn socially acceptable and personally satisfying ways of meeting their (normal) needs is the key to good parenting.* Below are a number of specific suggestions that should help you to become the best possible type of parent.

Few would debate that adolescence is a particularly stressful time. Adolescents have special concerns: relationships and being accepted by others; their identity—who they are and what their social role is (they usually try out several alternatives); what career or educational direction to choose; and becoming more independent and self-sufficient. These concerns, especially the last-mentioned, are often very difficult to achieve because adolescents simultaneously need their parents and resent having to be dependent on them. The so-called teenage rebellion is mostly related to this entirely normal quest for independence and the need to form an identity of their own. Adolescents are concerned about dating, romance and sex, and of course about having fun in ways that usually only youthful exuberance and energy can motivate. Youngsters are not "bad" in *what* they want, but sometimes in *how* they pursue their needs. They may frequently pursue their normal wants in ways that are self-destructive and even dangerous. Helping kids learn to help themselves in a manner that is acceptable is one of the major challenges of parenting. Alcohol is one of the important realities of growing up in today's world that parents must learn to confront and help their children deal with. Below are some tips that may help.

TIP 1: LOOK CLOSELY AT YOUR GOALS IN PARENTING

Take a moment to consider how you would like your children to develop, what personal qualities you value and are willing to help them acquire. Some of the characteristics that most parents want their children to achieve include: self-esteem; inner happiness;

self-confidence; self-protectiveness; self-sufficiency; self-control; an ability to understand themselves and others; self-discipline; and an ability to solve problems, to be responsive and to have trust in their parents. For a growing number of parents, fostering a broad sense of responsibility for the welfare of all inhabitants of the planet is an important quality they would like to see their children develop.

Realistically, no parent can expect a child to achieve all—or most—of these goals; they are just examples of the types of things one might want to work toward. If parents take the time to sort out what they feel are important qualities for a person to possess, they will have a sense of what they want for their children. As well, when they observe their children, they will be better equipped to see in which direction their child is moving. The more specific the goals, the easier it will be.

TIP 2: ARRANGE FOR ROUTINE FUN TIME TOGETHER

The notion that occasional "quality time" with your children will constitute an adequate job of parenting is simply not true. If you *regularly* spend "quality time" with your children—especially playful time—you will find that you kids will be much more open with you and will talk about almost any subject. Spending fun time together, especially when it's one-on-one, gives children the opportunity to really get to know you and feel comfortable with you under normal, positive conditions when you are not angry or trying to change some behavior of theirs. Generally speaking, the less parents talk and the more they listen, the more talking the children will do. When you are both enjoying yourselves together, it is not unusual for your children to bring up any topic that may be on their minds—drinking alcohol being just one of these possible subjects.

You can, of course, always raise questions yourself. Ask your kids their opinion about others who drink or, perhaps, how they feel about media advertising of alcohol, or even how they feel about someone in a movie who is drinking. Over time, this casual type of discussion about the subject of alcohol will enable you to discuss the topic in a natural, easy way that will not be mentioned only when a problem regarding alcohol arises. Remember, in order to have this kind of relationship with your children they will first have to like being with you, to trust you and respect you. So it is important to develop a friendship that extends beyond discipline. Do not wait for this essential relationship to occur on its own; make a point of establishing it and working at it.

TIP 3: FIND THINGS TO DO TOGETHER THAT YOU BOTH ENJOY

It is impossible to sustain any joint activity for very long unless both participants find pleasure in it. The activities you can consider doing together will naturally change as your kids get older. For example, you might be able to enjoy 5 to 10 minutes of playing with toys with a 3 year old, 20 minutes of playing catch with a 10 year old, or lunch at McDonald's or an afternoon of hiking or going to a ball game with a 17 year old. Obviously, you must decide what activities are age-appropriate and this will undoubtedly call for some creativity on your part. You have to take the time to come up with activities that will appeal to both of you. This kind of quality time spent with your children is one of the best times to exert influence on your children when you really need to.

TIP 4: LET CHILDREN MAKE SOME MISTAKES

Do not overrestrict, overprotect or overcontrol. At times you must refrain from interfering when you see that your child is about to make a mistake or even fail, because ultimately, learning the "hard way" is the best way. The trick is not to allow your children to experience failure that may be damaging to their physical or emotional welfare. The goal is to help them learn from bad experiences without seriously hurting themselves. If they fail, give them support and encourage them to get up and keep trying.

The following story is a good example of how to cope with your child's learning process. Tanya is a 15 1/2 year old who just got a learner's permit to drive. The law requires that when she drives she must always be accompanied by a licensed driver until she is 16, at which time she can apply for a regular license. Her mother deliberately makes a point of letting Tanya practice driving when they go for short trips on familiar roads, despite the fact that it takes more time, creates a greater risk of having an accident and requires listening to Tanya's frequent outbursts over her jerky gear changes with the stick shift. Her mother knows that each trip would be faster, safer and less hectic if she drove, but she realizes that in the long run, Tanya will be able to drive more skillfully and safely if she allows her to practice now. Tanya's mother restrains her urge to drive the car herself and says little about her daughter's numerous driving mistakes and hollering, choosing instead to let Tanya correct her own errors and improve her driving from her mistakes.

Another example concerns a mother whose son wants to learn how to cook. He likes to bake chocolate chip cookies, but does not want his mother to give him any help or offer any instructions. Instead of helping, which would be much easier, she allows him to do it his own way and find out by trial and error what his mistakes are. After several batches of burnt cookies and an extremely dirty kitchen (which he has to clean up himself), he learns how to become fairly independent and self-sufficient in the kitchen. Mom believes these skills will serve him well for the rest of his life, especially in today's world in which men frequently cook. The most important aspect of this story is clearly that the parent allows the child to take the time to learn without interfering and destroying a natural learning process.

TIP 5: TRY TO LISTEN AND UNDERSTAND YOUR CHILD'S PERSPECTIVES AND FEELINGS

Children, like adults, will inevitably experience periods of feeling bad; it's an unavoidable part of life. You must make a concerted effort to take their feelings seriously and keep in mind that what may seem like nothing to you may seem like the end of the world to your child. Try not to jump right in with all kinds of advice culled from "your years of experience." Do not try to "whip off" a solution; tell them "not to feel so bad" or what to do to avoid the same problem in the future. Likewise, it will not reduce your children's distress or emotional pain if you tell them they are overreacting and that the situation is not as bad as they are making it out to be. Just listen and give them your full attention. Stop doing what you are doing, look them in the eye, stand close and perhaps hug them if it seems appropriate. Silent moments are OK; it is not necessary for someone to be talking all the time. Careful, sympathetic listening alone is often enough to make youngsters feel better and may help them want to keep going, no matter how downtrodden or hopeless they feel. This type of non-judgmental, empathetic listening is an important part of developing the open, trusting relationship we have been talking about. You will want to make your children comfortable enough with you to want to tell you about their private thoughts and experiences. This will happen once they trust you and once you have a demonstrated record that you are a good listener and will not punish or belittle them for their mistakes. Being on the receiving end of your child's honest emotions will put you in a good position to help them to grow up feeling good about themselves and to become solid citizens. Of course, it doesn't always work out as well as you might like, so don't be disappointed with partial success. Ideal relationships are difficult to achieve.

TIP 6: LET KIDS LEARN RESPONSIBILITY THROUGH EXPERIENCE

Kids need to experience things themselves rather than just be told what is right and wrong, good and bad. To learn responsibility, they need to deal with the consequences of their actions. Knowing the rules of tennis, for example, doesn't make someone a good tennis player. Knowing the rules is quite different from learning the actual skills of how to play the game. The best way parents can help their children to learn responsibility is by letting them actually experience the natural ups and downs of daily life. An example of this type of learning follows. When one of the author's sons was 16 years old, he bought a car. His father often warned him about driving recklessly and especially about entering the driveway and the garage too fast. The boy paid little attention, but luckily fate intervened and succeeded in making a point where

Dad had failed. As he sped into the driveway one evening, the boy slightly clipped the edge of the garage door and as a result knocked off one of his car's bumper guards. The boy was furious with himself. The father, who was in the yard and had witnessed the whole incident, listened but did not say a word to his son's rantings and ravings. Succumbing to the temptation to say "I told you so" would likely have resulted in the boy getting angry with his father. The unhappy teenager paid for the damage to his car out of his meager earnings. Because Dad ignored his son's behavior after the incident and said nothing, letting fate be the teacher, this young man finally learned to drive more carefully.

TIP 7: RESCUE THEM WHEN THEY ARE CLEARLY OVER THEIR HEADS

Although it is best to let children learn from their experiences when there is no great danger involved, there *are* times to come to the rescue. When youngsters are unquestionably unable to solve a problem or make a decision because they are too young or inexperienced to perceive the possible danger or they have tried and failed and the problem persists, parents need to take the responsibility to help them out. An example of this type of circumstance is the account a friend of ours gave: his teenage son was working alone at a mini-mart when he was held up by two robbers with guns. One of the trembling gunmen instructed the boy to lie face down and held his weapon to the boy's head while the other robber cleared out the cash register. After the gunmen fled, the boss returned and said he would teach the lad how to use a .45 caliber handgun and supply him with a bullet-proof vest so that the next time he was held up he could take action. Recounting the experience to his parents, he wondered if the boss's plan would be OK. After his horrified parents caught their breath, they gave him their decision that they had made the instant they got the gist of the seriousness of the problem. The youngster simply wasn't able to perceive the enormous risk involved in what his boss wanted him to do, so his parents resolved the issue for him and told him in no uncertain terms that as of that moment he was unemployed and would have to find another job.

TIP 8:   BEHAVE IN WAYS YOU WANT THEM
TO BEHAVE

Author James Baldwin expressed it well: "Kids have never been good at listening to their elders, but they have never failed to imitate them." What he says is all too true; they are, indeed, much more likely to *do* what you do than what you *tell* them to do. For instance, if you, as a parent, drink too much, chances are your children, too, will tend to be excessive should they decide to drink. If you stage temper tantrums to get your way or punishment to gain control, your children will follow your example; however, if you are trying to understand someone else's perspective, and disagree politely in an argument, that is the behavior your kids will tend to imitate. What you advise your children to do has much less impact on what they actually see you demonstrate. Remember your own behavior is crucial to your child's behavior.

TIP 9:   USE POSITIVE NAMES AND LABELS
FOR YOUR KIDS

Be realistic—don't distort or falsify the truth, but note which things your children are good at doing, label them favorably and say something nice to the child about it: for example, "You're a good student. You get right down to work and do it right. I'm proud of you." Do *not* qualify your praise with something like, "Even though you get mostly As and Bs, you're a better student than that. Don't you think you could get all As next term?" Using positive names and labels will usually create a self-fulfilling prophecy, and so do negative ones. If you tell your son, "you are not much of a student and you have a bad temper," chances are he will not try any harder to be a better student because you don't expect it of him, and therefore he won't expect it of himself. He is more likely to have temper outbursts if both of you as his parents are anticipating this behavior and believe it will happen. And if you call your kid "stupid," "dumb," "worthless," or worse, you should not be surprised if he performs exactly along those lines. Some behavioral scientists consider such name-calling to be a form of child abuse since it can hurt for a lifetime.

TIP 10: BE GENEROUS WITH YOUR PRAISE AND ENCOURAGEMENT

Instead of waiting for the inevitable mistakes your children will make, note what they do well and let them know frequently how much you approve. Be the opposite of the "warden," described in Step 1, who always looks for things to complain about. Instead, be a "positive teacher"; when you see your kids doing the right thing reward them immediately with your attention and praise. (This outlook of systematic approval will make you a rare commodity in today's world, whether you practice it on the job, at home, with kids or with adults.)

   If you can, participate in your kids' prosocial or constructive activities. For example, while you should not do their homework for them, it's a good idea to show interest in what they have to do. Maybe they are reading a book for school that you read years ago and wouldn't mind reading again so you can talk with them about it from a position of recent knowledge and genuine interest. Such interaction and attention are usually very well received by most kids and will encourage them to pursue whatever activity it is you are sharing, such as the enjoyment of a book. Like playing together, having common interests not only encourages that activity by rewarding it with your attention, but also creates the type of relationship needed for dealing with troublesome issues, like drinking.

TIP 11: REWARD THEIR PROGRESS IN GRADUAL STEPS

Don't expect kids to do exactly what you want the first time just because you told them what you want and how you want them to do it. This applies to everything: getting better at controlling their anger; not picking on a younger sibling as much; getting better grades; making better decisions; and politely disagreeing in stating their point of view. To use just one of these examples, "No, Mom, I see it differently. I think it's just too much trouble to collect bottles and cans for recycling. It just doesn't pay enough and I think it's a waste of time to bother with it." Compare that type of response with, "You're wrong about that, Mom. It's just plain stupid to recycle stuff and you're really dumb to do it." When they show *any* improvement, praise their progress even though they may be far from where you'd like them to be. Remember that improvement is a slow and gradual process—you may have to pay close attention to see improvement, but if it's there it means you and your child are on the right track. Keep attending to and rewarding those small steps toward sound behavior.

TIP 12: PICK YOUR PRIORITIES

It's a bottomless pit to struggle with your kids to control or influence every little thing they do. Select your issues very carefully. You only have so much energy and so much influence, and your impact will be much greater if you don't fight every battle. You want to win wars, not skirmishes (it is like going for checkmate rather than winning pieces in a chess game). The ultimate goal in the context of this book is for your kids to make good decisions about alcohol while they grow up to be happy and well adjusted. There is no point in struggling to control them at every step to prove that you are the boss. It really is no contest when we compare the significance of wearing crazy hair with the importance of getting drunk, or having a messy room with driving safely.

TIP 13: IGNORE RATHER THAN PUNISH
MINOR, UNWANTED BEHAVIOR

Kids do a great many things their parents don't really like. If the issue is minor (clothes, hair style, messy desk), you are usually better off ignoring them. This may be hard to do, but save your energy for the important things. No reaction at all has some effect in discouraging the behavior, especially if your attention is a reward and that is usually the case. Kids may act up as a way of getting parental attention, but if you use your interest and attention to strengthen desirable behaviors and are not stingy about it, they will have little need to resort to obnoxious behavior as a way of getting your valuable attention.

TIP 14: USE PUNISHMENT SPARINGLY

Any use of punishment carries with it certain risks. Parents are most often motivated to use punishment because of anger—they are acting aggressively toward a child who has angered them. Such punishment is not merely limited in its effectiveness in getting rid of the unwanted behavior, it usually only provokes anger and avoidance in the child. For punishment to be most effective, parents must be in control of themselves and matter-of-factly impose punishment that has previously been discussed with and understood by the child. Generally speaking, the best kind of punishment is removal of privileges or other desirable things (going out on weekends for example). Physical and verbal punishment (such as hitting or name calling) should *rarely if ever* be used except, perhaps, to prevent life-threatening behavior such as swatting a 4 year old for walking out onto the street. Moreover, for punishment to really work, you have to carry it out every time the undesirable behavior occurs—and this can be very difficult. Also, to continue to have an effect, the severity of punishment may have to be increased over time, which can become very unpleasant for everyone involved, including you. In addition, punishment makes children feel bad about themselves and angry at the person dispensing it. It is subjectively unpleasant, and it models aversive power control over others and hence encourages your child to use it on others. For example, children who frequently get physically or verbally punished by their parents are more likely to hit, slap, or yell at brothers, sisters or friends as a means of controlling them. Also, parental use of physical punishment can escalate to the point of losing emotional control and, in extreme cases, physical abuse. For example, look at the result of one case we are aware of: a father who frequently beat up his son got a bit of his own medicine. When the son got old enough and big enough, he beat up his father, and that finally ended the abuse. The use of punishment frequently results in a child's avoidance of the punisher (your daughter may not act rude in your presence anymore, but she also avoids being around you). When a parent tells us, "I don't know what's wrong with that kid of mine—I never see him, he never stays at home," we have to wonder just what happens when he *is* at home.

Keep in mind that mild and fair punishment may be helpful when it guides children toward alternative positive behaviors that can then be rewarded ("Because you came home late tonight, you can't go out tomorrow night, but I will give you another chance the next night to see if you can make it home on time").

Spelling out and delivering clear consequences for bad behavior can save a lot of wasted talk and energy if you do it right. The consequence of a child's action must be appropriate to the infraction. The following examples are appropriate to minor infractions: coming home late may result in losing the privilege of going out for one day; failure to do homework may result in the loss of going out for the weekend, loss of telephone privileges, going to parties or use of the family car. Loss of privileges should not last for too long; usually a few days is sufficient. A week seems like a very long time to an adolescent, and only major and repeated violations justify a week or possibly two weeks of restriction or loss of privileges. In addition, it's a good idea to let teenagers earn their privileges back early when they show some special effort. Perhaps they can do extra chores like cleaning the garage or doing yard work or painting. This way young people will understand that when they act in a certain way they will face certain consequences. You must make your stance clear to your children. *Never* say "because I told you so." They should not feel resentful if you've explained your reasons for punishing them and make it clear that it is not particularly easy for you either. To summarize, see unwanted behavior for what it is, punish sparingly and when you must punish, use an appropriate method that will help and not just hurt.

TIP 15: ENCOURAGE ACTIVITIES

The busier kids are, especially with constructive things, the better. They are less likely to get bored and do silly, worthless and potentially risky things like spending too much time partying and getting drunk. Try to get them involved in a wide range of activities. You can help by being willing to drive them, pay for expenses and perhaps help them arrange getting involved. Busy kids are not as likely to drink or use drugs out of boredom or undirected restless energy.

TIP 16: SET LIMITS AND SPECIFY CONSEQUENCES

Kids need to know that there are limits to what they can do. Clearly, reasonable limits will not provoke as much rebellion or argument as harsh ones do. In order for your children to follow your rules, you must negotiate and reach a mutually satisfactory agreement on which specific behaviors will provoke consequences. Be precise and consistent so that your child knows exactly what you consider unacceptable behavior and what the consequences will be if they ignore the family rules. To reinforce your kids' adherence to your limit-setting, you can, for example, offer a bonus allowance for a week of coming home on time every day, or losing a weekend night out for being late two nights in one week.

TIP 17: TEACH KIDS TO DISAGREE POLITELY AND TO HAVE THEIR OWN OPINION

If you expect your children to handle the encouragement and perhaps overt pressure to drink, they will need a considerable amount of experience and practice in courteously asserting themselves, especially if it means disagreeing with others. That means they need *you* as a role model to learn how to conduct themselves in a situation of this sort. Knowing that they *should* say no to drugs and alcohol and having the motivation, skill and self-confidence to actually do so are two different things entirely. They have to learn the skills of polite, but assertive refusal. Then, they have to learn how to stick to the decision. This takes practice and the acceptance by adults of their right to an opinion and the right to express it even if it contradicts the opinion of a parent. You are their teacher. Don't take it personally if they err by being too blunt or not polite enough while learning to disagree without being rude or loud. You might have to say, "Son, I respect your right to your own opinion. You don't have to shout or be defensive. Try to express yourself more tactfully." If you want them to make their own decisions about alcohol and not to be swayed by others, help them learn how to confront others' views by starting the process at home. Where else are they going to learn it? Their peers certainly aren't going to offer them much, if any, opportunity for nonconformity. Therefore, they will need patient, objective feedback from you so they can correct their errors and hone their ability to make their own decisions. Praise them for any improvement. They have to learn *how* to do what they need to do.

TIP 18:   ARRANGE SPECIAL OUTINGS

An example of a special reward that simultaneously strengthens a behavior you like, provides pleasurable interaction for everyone and encourages your child to have contact with the kinds of friends you consider to be a positive influence, is to arrange special outings. Let's say a special outing is contingent upon your child having been especially good about schoolwork or getting along with siblings. When a reward such as a special outing follows a behavior pattern you are trying to encourage, that behavior is more likely to continue in the future. If the outing is something everybody likes, it is also a great time for playing together and fostering the positive relationship for influencing children that we talked about earlier. In addition, you can selectively encourage contact with a particular friend of theirs, one that you enjoy and think is a good influence, by suggesting that he or she come along on the outing.

HOW TO USE THESE EXAMPLES

To make some of these guidelines more meaningful, it will help you to consider a common example of a teenager's encounter with alcohol. Suppose your normally well-behaved, 17-year-old daughter with whom you have a reasonably open relationship tells you that she drank two beers last Friday night in the parking lot after the football game. One of the boys had a twelvepack that his older brother had bought for him. Despite her repeated refusal to have any, she finally gave in to her friend's pressure to have one since she wanted to feel accepted. She drank one and then another. She rode home with someone who had also been drinking. Now she feels regret and is ashamed, but has decided to tell you about it anyway. What should you do? Consider how you might use some of the suggestions in this chapter to deal with the problem. Think about it before you read the following comments and recommendations.

The very fact that your daughter would tell you about her drinking episode is a good indication that you have a positive relationship with her. It suggests in the past you have tolerated her mistakes without having overreacted to them or having imposed harsh and probably ineffective punishments. The first thing to do is to carefully listen to exactly what happened and how she feels about it. Try hard to control your first reactions and feelings. Let her tell the whole story and give her plenty of time and perhaps assistance to understand her own feeling about what happened. Only after she has finished saying what she has to say should you express your disapproval; to begin by voicing your concern about her welfare would be a good idea. Let her know that you are upset about what happened because you love her and don't want her to get hurt, or for her to hurt anyone else. Do not immediately react by threatening her with punishment and try hard not to lose control of your temper by being abusive or overly angry. To punish her for what she did will only alienate and discourage her from telling you about any future drinking situations or experiences. Instead, assist her to figure out a better way of dealing with the same situation should it arise again. Tell her that she should stand her ground; if she does not want to drink, and this is what has been decided by the family, she should not and under no circumstances should she give in to peer pressure. If her friends have all been drinking and if she needs a ride, she should call home. It is also acceptable if she can find a ride home with someone who has not been drinking. If you find it necessary—and often it is not—you could tell her that any future form of drinking will result in some form of mild punishment. However, failure to tell you about any future drinking incidents that you might find out about, will result in more severe consequences (such as grounding for a week). In this way, she is still likely to continue to tell you about other situations regarding drinking, which preserves your access to her experiences, while drinking and trying to keep it from you is relatively less likely. Using punishment in this way can be effective when combined with praise and approval for the good things she does, such as coming home sober and on time, or possibly dealing effectively with other problematic behavior. If you can create and maintain a close and open relationship with her, your chances of knowing about her future experiences and being able to influence them are much greater.

The foregoing example uses several of the suggestions we have listed above for maximizing daily influence on your children that will ultimately translate into their behavior as adults: (1) a history of open communication between you and your child and when punishment is necessary, making sure it fits the incident; (2) good times together that foster trust and mutually positive feelings; (3) tolerance of mistakes and a chance to correct them; (4) careful listening; (5) expressing your love and concern for them even though you disapprove of this particular behavior; (6) not overreacting; (7) being reticent regarding the benefits of punishment; and (8) providing realistic ways of making better decisions. Reacting in these ways will not drive children underground, causing them to keep things from you in the future. It is critical for you, as parents, to work on maintaining access to your kids if you want to be able to influence them. This approach stands in contrast to the parental role of the rule-enforcer who, not knowing what to do, acts impulsively, angrily and inconsistently. As stated before, you need a game plan and a set of prior guidelines in order to do the job right.

You should apply these principles and strategies to your own personal efforts as a parent as well. You, too, are going to make mistakes. It has been stated that parenting does not come naturally. You will lose your temper and be punitive at times, or inconsistent and model the wrong kind of behavior. Don't expect instant perfection from yourself any more than you expect it from children. Forgive yourself and keep on trying. You will improve in gradual steps. Review these guidelines periodically and continue to practice using them.

One final thought. Many years from now, when you are older and your children have grown up, you may become dependent on them in many ways. Respecting them now, when they are young, will increase the likelihood of their treating you the same way when you need them. Most children never forget.

PART 2

Taking Action

The four steps in Part 2 deal with decisions about drinking, fostering nondrinking behavior, teaching sensible drinking (if nondrinking fails) and handling teenage alcohol abuse. Here, we suggest ways to get the entire family involved in an exploration of the role of alcohol. We have found that this knowledge is essential in order to clarify family values about drinking. The ultimate goal is to reach a fully thought-out decision about the use of alcohol that everyone in the family can live with—parents and children alike—and to provide guidelines for carrying out that decision in a rational manner. For those families who decide that they do not want their teenagers to drink, we suggest ways for parents to offer support that will help them abstain. Often this means that parents must help their kids learn how to successfully buck peer pressure and avoid problems, especially with persuasive friends. This area clearly must address the issue of driving under the influence. For those parents who decide that their teenager is allowed to drink, but only under certain conditions, we provide ways to improve the chances that their children will drink sensibly and ways that they can minimize the risks of getting into trouble. Finally, alcohol abuse is addressed since it is a hazard faced by everyone who drinks. Parents are alerted to those signs that indicate teenage alcohol abuse and are provided with strategies for active intervention.

Step 4

Making Decisions about Drinking

Taking into consideration the age and maturity of your teenager, and the reality that he may already be drinking, you will need to make a decision about whether or not you sanction drinking of any kind or prefer that he not use alcohol at all. Once you and your spouse have come to a decision on this matter and have decided how you wish to influence your child's decisions about drinking, you can then consider using some of the suggestions given below. There are many factors involved in decisions about drinking. As parents you will want to maximize your input to influence as many of these factors as you can so that your teenagers' drinking decisions will be compatible with your family values about alcohol or at the very least so they know the facts. To clarify your own values about the appropriate role of alcohol, consider some of the pros and cons of drinking:

Reasons Not to Drink	*Reasons to Drink*
1. Long-term health risk	1. It feels good
2. In most states it's against the law	2. It tastes good
3. Negative effect on judgment and thought	3. It relaxes
4. Risk of drunk-driving	4. By relaxing inhibitions, it aids in socializing
5. Reduces emotional control	5. It alters your mental or emotional state

6. Interferes with restorative sleep
7. Risk of a hangover

6. Some alcoholic beverages go well with food
7. Plays a significant role in some religious and family celebrations

8. Risk of impulsive sexual behavior
9. Risk of eventual abuse
10. Can cause marital and other relationship problems

8. Gives a brief respite from the daily grind

MODELING

Your children have been watching you since they were born. If you are a nondrinker, they too will more likely be nondrinkers. If you are a light or moderate drinker, they should have acquired some sense of what moderate drinking is and if they choose to drink, hopefully they will model their drinking habits on yours. By the same token, if you are a heavy drinker, your behavior may very possibly have influenced them to become excessive drinkers. It is also quite possible that your behavior has had the opposite effect—they don't want to drink at all, especially if your kids have had bad experiences with your drinking. Since modeling is a proven influence on behavior, one important way you may be able to influence your children's drinking decisions is to model non-use or the responsible use of alcohol.

EXPECTATIONS ABOUT THE EFFECTS OF ALCOHOL

What kids believe alcohol will do for them influences their decision to drink, how much they drink and how they will behave while drinking. If kids believe that alcohol enhances their ability to relate to the opposite sex, to be more competent and successful, and provides a handy excuse for acting out without risk of censure, then they are more likely to become drinkers and to abuse alcohol. On the other hand, if they have accurate knowledge of the effects of alcohol (a mild social lubricant that produces a brief and very modest euphoria along with varying degrees of impairment in most performance abilities, not to mention painful hangovers), they will not be as inclined to use or abuse alcohol. Learning the truth and correcting expectancies about the effects of alcohol is a significant way for parents to influence their children's eventual choices.

KNOWLEDGE ABOUT ALCOHOL

Being knowledgeable about alcohol gives both teens and adults a better base for making their own rational decisions about drinking. How much do teens already know about alcohol and what do they need to know? A recent survey of teens carried out by the authors reflected just what you might expect: they are quick to pronounce warnings about drinking ("It breaks up marriages and families"), they demonstrate profound misunderstandings ("A glass of wine a day prevents cancer") and they recognize the fact of widespread use and abuse ("Teenagers drink a lot at parties and they get out of control"). In Step 2 we reviewed the essential facts about alcohol required for making informed decisions. Parents need to find out what their kids know and don't know, correct misunderstandings and fill in the gaps. To increase your leverage and influence on their choices about alcohol, we will suggest a number of specific approaches you can try. They will be presented in order of difficulty from easier and less threatening to those that may be more emotionally charged and thus harder to carry out. Parents will have to assess their child's level of maturity, knowledge and experience and adapt their approach accordingly. The subject may come up spontaneously or parents can raise it at a family meeting called specifically to express concern about alcohol and drinking. One way to break the ice is to tell them that you are aware of teenage drinking statistics that show that the majority of teens experiment with alcohol and often have opportunities to drink. Parents might wish to present some of the statistics on teen drinking from Step 1 to back up their reasons for concern.

EXPLORING YOUR FAMILY DRINKING HISTORY

The reason for starting with your family's history is that it allows you to ease into the topic by talking about relatives outside your immediate family. In many families there are a variety of drinking styles. It can be interesting and fun to compare observations and introduce ideas about drinking choices and sensible drinking habits. A history of serious drinking problems within a family suggests a significant risk factor for young people in that family, particularly males. It may be that there is a hereditary factor being transmitted or it may be that social structures within families are conducive to teaching and passing on abusive behavior; no one knows for sure. If good old uncle Walt, as well as Grandpa Claude, had a long-term serious problem with alcohol, their young relatives should know about it and be aware that they may be at a somewhat greater risk than other people—that is, if they choose to drink. And if Mom or Dad have serious alcohol problems, or did in the past, the risk factor is even greater.

DRINK WATCHING

First, ask your kids what they personally have observed about the changes that take place in people's behavior when they drink—whether at family gatherings, parties, in restaurants, or at dinner with friends. If they have been around teens who were drinking, what happened? (But don't quiz them for information about their friends, as this could cause resentment and cause them to clam up.) Plan ahead with kids for opportunities to watch others drink. Tell them to be observant so you can discuss what they saw later. Some of the things you can tell them to look for are: how people drink (gulping versus sipping), how many drinks they consume, how their behavior and emotions change, and whether they become more or less pleasant. When people are obviously drinking abusively, what happens to them? Watch for any signs of extreme emotion, such as becoming tearful, hostile or withdrawn. How do others react to them? Do they notice a difference in those who have only a couple of drinks? Do their behavior and emotions change? Do people act responsibly when they drink, are they courteous, do they drive despite being incapacitated, are they trying to make decisions that they clearly are in no position to make? Try to find a chance to talk with your children during the event to point out how certain people are drinking and behaving. "Did you notice that man over there gulping down his drinks? His wife isn't drinking at all and she doesn't seem to like what he's doing." "The woman in the green dress seems to be a very moderate drinker and seems to be able to maintain an attitude of politeness and cheerfulness." Such observations can easily be tied to the factual material presented in Step 2, such as blood alcohol level and behavior change, healthy versus unhealthy drinking styles and the importance of eating while drinking.

WORKING OUT A DRUNK-DRIVING AGREEMENT

For most parents of teens, concern about drunk driving and possible accidents is a primary fear, as well it should be—alcohol-related car wrecks are the leading cause of death for teenagers and young adults. Teens should be aware that there is a particular blood alcohol level cutoff in each state for "driving under the influence." Find out what the law is in your state and be sure your teen knows what it is. They need to know the penalties for drunk driving and the fact that any alcohol in the blood impairs driving ability. There is no "safe" drinking and driving zone; impairment of coordination begins at a BA of 20—about one drink for most people. To have an even stronger impact on the emotional significance and seriousness of drinking and driving, parents can consider doing three other things. First, go see for yourself some form of the trauma caused by drunk driving. Many cities have safety programs that include presentations by accident victims who survived serious injury caused by a drunk driver, or personal accounts of the loss suffered by the relatives of people who died because of drunk driving. To see and hear these victims in person describe real personal tragedies has far more emotional impact than just hearing about them. MADD (Mothers Against Drunk Driving) sponsors such activities as do some alcohol treatment centers and local law enforcement agencies. It's a good idea to call around and track down something like this so your child can experience it. Some of the existing films are pretty frightening, but they do the trick. A second possibility is to check into programs that some cities have begun which require high school students caught driving under the influence to visit the city morgue and see the dead body of a drunk-driving victim, including a visual encounter with dissected bodies. The experience has a profound emotional effect upon those who participate but, again, it works. A third possibility is to rent an educational video on the topic, such as *Drunk Driving: The Toll, The Tears*, watch it with your teenager, then discuss it. These, too, can be hard-hitting, so be sure to watch it first to make certain it is what you expect. It's better to avoid using anything your teen has already seen at school, since that makes it more likely they will tune out. After discussing your concern, and once you have come to some sort of mutual agreement on the potential problems of drinking, present and discuss the SADD Contract for Life. Treat it as an important, serious legal document to be signed with solemnity. This contract was developed by Students Against Driving Drunk and its widespread use has proved to be an effective preventive measure to keep teens from needlessly being involved in alcohol-related car accidents. It is reprinted here with the permission of SADD, and can be copied right off the page and blown up to a larger size. Once it is signed, consider framing and hanging it in the house as a constant reminder that the contract exists and must be adhered to at all times.

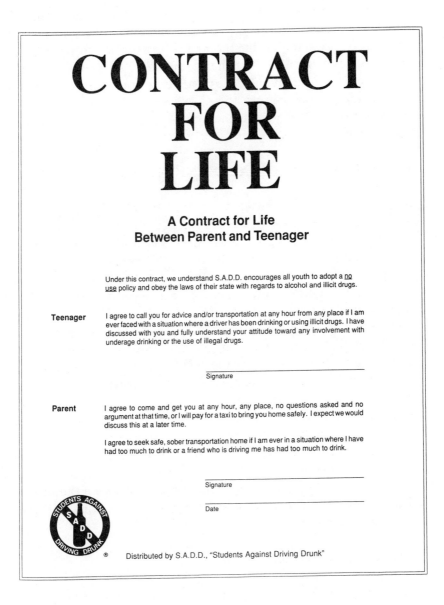

CONTRACT FOR LIFE

A Contract for Life
Between Parent and Teenager

Under this contract, we understand S.A.D.D. encourages all youth to adopt a no use policy and obey the laws of their state with regards to alcohol and illicit drugs.

Teenager   I agree to call you for advice and/or transportation at any hour from any place if I am ever faced with a situation where a driver has been drinking or using illicit drugs. I have discussed with you and fully understand your attitude toward any involvement with underage drinking or the use of illegal drugs.

_____
Signature

Parent   I agree to come and get you at any hour, any place, no questions asked and no argument at that time, or I will pay for a taxi to bring you home safely. I expect we would discuss this at a later time.

I agree to seek safe, sober transportation home if I am ever in a situation where I have had too much to drink or a friend who is driving me has had too much to drink.

_____
Signature

_____
Date

Distributed by S.A.D.D., "Students Against Driving Drunk"

We emphasize the formal use of the SADD contract; research has shown that children and adults are more likely to keep a promise if they actually sign their name to a formal document that spells out specifically what that promise is, as opposed to just agreeing to it verbally. (A recurrent suggestion throughout this book is for you, as parents, to use every bit of available leverage in order to influence your teenagers—so take the extra trouble to use written contracts.)

DISCUSSING THE LEGAL DRINKING AGE

Many teens consider the legal age of 21 for drinking to be out of touch with the reality of the lives of young people. That they feel this way about the law is a good indication of how likely they are to be drinkers before they turn 21. If, for example, your teenage daughter regards the law as "idiotic" and then tells you that she plans to follow it by abstaining until she is of legal age, you can share the joke with her but ask her to "get real." Maturing teens need to know that you understand their desire to be treated as adults, to enjoy the full privileges that adulthood brings. They may be curious to hear about your own struggle with the "legal age" issue when you were their age and if you felt the same way then as they do now. You may want to discuss strategies for handling it during the coming years. Some kids may openly express their intention to drink in violation of the law; others may feel opposed to it, but plan to obey for fear of legal repercussions. Others may plan never to drink at all, and therefore the age limit is of no importance to them. In any case, if you can find out your teenager's honest opinion about the current drinking law, it will help you deal more effectively with questions about their drinking.

TAKING A SKID ROW TOUR

The material in Step 7 will give you a good factual introduction to the complex area of alcohol abuse and plenty of topics for you to discuss with your teenagers. You need to make clear your worry that they might eventually become abusers of alcohol, and here again some direct involvement with them (such as a field trip) will be likely to have more impact than just a discussion. You could, for example, take a drive or a walk with your teenager through a part of town where many cheap bars and alcohol-dependent people are to be found. It can be an impressive lesson in the unhappy outcome of severe alcohol problems. You can comment that most of these people probably once had jobs, families, relationships and good health, all of which were damaged by abusive drinking. It is indeed a depressing and sad sight, but it is a reality—and an all-too-common part of life that many people never witness.

CONSIDERING ALCOHOL AND DRUGS IN GENERAL

Most teens have discussed with other kids why alcohol and tobacco are legal, yet other substances that may not be as hazardous are illegal (particularly marijuana). Explore everyone's attitudes and opinions in your family about legal and illegal substances, the risks involved in breaking the law to experiment with drugs, and the specific and relative hazards of cocaine, amphetamines, marijuana and heroin. It is extremely important that you know what you are talking about—your kids will be far more apt to listen to you if you are well-informed. To facilitate discussion you might rent a videotape of *Drugstore Cowboy, Sid and Nancy* or *The Boost,* watch it together, then discuss what you saw. Specifically, how did taking drugs affect the characters, their ability to work, to think straight, to relate to others and their propensity for getting into trouble? Because the language and situations are pretty raw in all three of these films, they may not be appropriate for younger children, but most teens are used to hearing rough language and will not likely be shocked by it. In fact, they will probably be worried that *you* will be shocked since teens often imagine that their parents are as naive as parents like to think their teens are.

EVALUATING TEEN DRINKING OR
POTENTIAL DRINKING

In the course of carrying out some of the suggestions above, you may have already discovered whether or not your child has tried alcohol, currently is a drinker, or has even become an abuser. If you do not already know about their drinking habits (if any), now is the time to ask them more directly about their own use, as well as their opinions on drinking in general. Do they drink now? Have they ever? With whom? How much? Where? It may take a bit of patient inquiry to get the truth. Avoid coming on to them like a police interrogator because it will most likely make them clam up. Try not to respond emotionally if they tell you about some drinking experiences unknown to you; if you respond with anger or if you act devastated about something that jars you, chances are they will not be inclined to be honest with you in the future.

Sometimes a teenager's drinking comes to the attention of parents because of their behavior. A good example is the case of Liz, a mature and well-behaved 16 year old. Her parents had always assumed she was so totally trustworthy that they could leave her at home alone when they went out of town. Drinking had not been discussed at length in this family because it had never been an issue, and there was an unspoken understanding between Liz and her parents that she was not to drink (although she had tried alcohol in the company of her parents).

Nonetheless, the combination of absent parents, a temporarily empty house and persuasive friends made Liz decide to throw a party. When her parents came back the next day, they noticed a suspicious stain on the carpet and asked about it. Liz's unconvincing reply was that she had a couple of friends over and one of them spilled a soda. She said it was "just a soft drink or juice or something." A sniff of the spot, however, suggested otherwise and caused her parents to look further into the situation. Lo and behold, the trash container outside the house contained several beer cans and an empty vodka bottle.

So as not to spoil the future utility of trash inspection as a source of evidence, Liz's parents didn't mention their findings, but continued questioning her with a doubting attitude. This eventually led to Liz's gradual and begrudging disclosure of the drinking episode. Initially her story was that just a couple of friends were over and they each had a beer or two. Her parents' continued probing and the fact that they were obviously irritated by having to continue to dig out the truth from her sketchy and ambiguous account eventually resulted in an increasingly descriptive confession; there had, in fact, been a party with at least 10 people and plenty of drinking (the trash-can evidence could have been used if necessary).

This case of lying by a normally honest and trustworthy teenager is fairly typical of teenage drinking without parental involvement. The combination of social coercion by friends and the temptation of an empty house on a Saturday night caused Liz to do something she ordinarily wouldn't have done; she threw an unmonitored party where many of the participants drank abusively. Her parents, by the way, could have been sued if someone had been injured or if there had been a car accident in which the driver admitted that he had been drinking at Liz's parents' house.

It should be quite clear that a family cannot communicate about drinking or negotiate a viable set of family rules about alcohol without knowledge of what their kids' current drinking habits are.

FAMILY VALUES ABOUT DRINKING

It is recommended that a family have an open discussion between all members about alcohol and its role in daily life. These facts can help lay the groundwork for establishing a set of explicit family rules about drinking, providing an opportunity to clarify any significant differences of opinion, and can help your family to find some reasonable common ground that everyone can live with. It can be helpful for parents who are comfortable with self-disclosure to set an example by talking about their own reasons for drinking or not drinking. If you are a nondrinker, you can explain to your teen how that came to be. If you are a drinker, you may wish to discuss your current drinking and the reasons and values behind it.

NEGOTIATING A SET OF FAMILY RULES ON DRINKING

By this point you should make sure you know enough about your teen's habits and attitudes toward drinking that you can work out a set of rules. Parents should not simply draw up a list of rules, demand compliance from their teens and force them to obey. If you make the rules on your own, the contract will be one-sided and will most likely be ignored because the teenagers were not included; their input is essential so that the rules you decide on are ones that they can live with and will obey. A contract should include the following items:

1. Whether or not your teen will drink at all.

2. If they drink, where will they do it (at home with parents only, at supervised parties, at family gatherings)?

3. How much drinking is acceptable?

4. Transportation arrangements must be made whenever your child drinks away from home.

5. The consequences of violating these rules.

The age and maturity of your teenager should be considered in determining the specifics of the contract. The first contract you draw up probably will be far from perfect and may have to be renegotiated. Contracts between parents and teens need periodic updating and probably should automatically be reviewed every 6 months, or be able to be called up for review at any time by any family member.

Opposite is an example of what a typical contract might look like for a family with a drinking teen. It is adapted to fit the values and beliefs of that particular family—something you, too, should do.

BARNES FAMILY CONTRACT ON DRINKING

- Tom will be allowed to drink only with parental approval to be determined on each occasion and with at least one parent present. Under these conditions a maximum of two drinks is allowed.

- When out with friends, Tom will refuse all drinks offered to him and ignore any encouragement to change his mind.

- If a drinking and driving situation arises, no matter what the cause, Tom will follow the SADD guidelines and call home for assistance.

- When in the company of family members, Tom will not drink without asking for parental permission and will not argue if he is told "no" at that time.

Evidence of the violation of any of the above rules will result in a family meeting that will be held within 24 hours to determine the appropriate response. Consequences may include: loss of driving privileges, work detail, grounding, social restriction or reduction in the "quarterly fund for sober behavior."

Date_____   Signatures_____

_____

Of course, a contract such as this one cannot guarantee that Tom will *never* drink without his parents' supervision. It does make it clear, however, that such drinking will not be condoned and that to do it would mean that Tom doesn't care about going back on his signed promise, taking the risk of being caught and facing the consequences. It is probably realistic to assume that on occasion he may drink with other teens, but he will at least think seriously about doing it each time an opportunity occurs. And hopefully, he will usually opt to turn down those chances to drink.

As a final matter of concern, we must address parents' understandably strong, negative emotions about the idea of their children experimenting with drugs and/or alcohol. It is only natural for them to worry that their kids could get hooked, end up with terrible emotional problems and perhaps even a com-

pletely ruined life if they become abusers. Parents should understand, however, that experimentation does not guarantee disaster.
If it did, we would be living in a world filled with burned-out
zombies since most typical teens will experiment to some degree
with alcohol. A recent 20-year study of youthful drug and alcohol
use revealed something interesting: Those young people who
abused drugs or alcohol as teenagers or as young adults typically
had been identified very early in life as emotionally disturbed
children. However, the healthiest, most well-adjusted young
adults had usually done some drug and alcohol experimentation
during their teen years. It is noteworthy that those who had *never*
experimented during their teens were *not* the healthiest and most
well-adjusted young adults. Instead, they tended to be more
inhibited, fearful of authority and less able to make use of their
own initiative or imagination. A plausible interpretation of the
results of this study is that teenagers who are *already* maladjusted
are the ones who are more likely to drift into drug and alcohol
abuse, rather than drug and alcohol abuse somehow being the
cause of their maladjustment. So don't let the discovery of your
child's minor drug or alcohol experimentation alarm you too
greatly. It may mean nothing more than that he or she is a normal,
curious and maturing individual, learning about the world
through trial and error, as we must do.

Step 5

Helping Teens Abstain

Many teenagers have not made a decision about drinking and over one-third do not drink. If family and friends are primarily nondrinkers and have reasonably stable and satisfying lives that may include contact with drinkers, the chances that your children, too, will abstain are pretty good. The reason that it is important to include drinkers in your ring of social contacts is that the majority of people do in fact drink, and unless there is at least occasional interaction with drinkers, teens will not be prepared to successfully maintain a nondrinking lifestyle in a social environment that will inevitably include opportunities and encouragement to drink.

As discussed already, there are many good reasons not to drink. It can interfere with school work, job performance, athletic ability, social skills, personal relationships, sleep, sexual ability, health and weight management, and energy to do other things in life. And for some people, drinking may be counter to their religious or social values.

If drinking serves no positive function or purpose for someone—enhancing socializing, relaxing, or ceremonial use— and the individual enjoys many satisfying activities without it, there is probably little or no inclination to begin drinking. Some of the people in the 30 percent of the adult population who don't drink feel this way. For others, alcoholic beverages may not be compatible with their health or with personal, religious, family, or peer group values. Some do not like the taste, smell, or effects of alcohol, and for these reasons they choose not to drink. Yet others may come from families where certain members have had a history of alcohol problems, so they make a conscious decision not to drink to avoid any possibility of developing a similar problem.

Today it is easier than it was in the past not to follow what others or even the majority of society are doing, whether this means smoking, eating red meat, or drinking. No longer are adults as pressured to do what most others are doing when it comes to personal habits. That change has thankfully left adults freer to decide what is best for them and to develop personal habits that suit them, as individuals, not the majority of society.

Of course, there is still social encouragement from others to drink. Direct or subtle influences to do as others do are and always will be present, but at least adults aren't expected to conform to the behavior of the majority in order to be accepted or else be regarded and treated as an oddball. Unfortunately, this freedom adults feel to follow their own inclinations is not true for teenagers. It is important to remember that teenagers' intense desire for social acceptance is much more important than it is for older people, and they are subjected to peer pressure far more than adults are. Thus, life for teenagers is far more difficult with regard to resisting social encouragement to drink.

Fortunately, society has taken a more active and outspoken role that makes it easier to choose not to drink and then to carry out that decision. Social policies and other influences today often discourage drinking. We have raised the legal drinking age back to 21 in those states where it was lowered. We have enacted tougher drunk driving laws and made penalties more severe for driving under the influence. In public drinking establishments, liquor stores and on alcoholic beverage containers we read notices warning that drinking causes birth defects, that alcohol consumption is dangerous if you are operating equipment or driving, and that it may be bad for your health. Mothers Against Drunk Driving (MADD) and Students Against Driving Drunk (SADD) are active and influential organizations that offer frequent media coverage. In recent years the government's influential alcohol research bureau, the National Institute on Alcohol Abuse and Alcoholism, has taken a conservative stance and seems to emphasize abstinence and support for policy changes that would reduce the availability of alcoholic beverages and impose higher taxes on their sale. The alcohol industry itself has shown increasing concern about the abuse of its products and has spent millions of dollars on public awareness programs. Professional sports organizations such as the National Basketball Association and the National Football League have also spent considerable sums of money to discourage alcohol and drug abuse.

Overall, the tenor of the messages we get today about drinking is that you don't have to drink, but if you do, be careful about it. And if you drink too much, be prepared to suffer severe consequences for it. This is no secret and most teenagers are very aware of these messages.

One entertaining way to become more aware of the changes that have taken place in our social habits is to watch old movies. In some ways, movies chronicle the way we were at different times in our history, and the changes you will see in drinking and smoking habits are glaring and often amusing. Film characters drank and smoked without ceasing in movies made in the '30s, '40s and '50s. Practically every time someone came into a room where others were gathered, they were immediately offered a drink or otherwise just poured themselves one. How often have you heard someone say "I need a drink" in an older movie? In fact, in some of those films there is rarely a scene that doesn't include everyone sloshing down a drink, often with a kind of desperation that suggests taking pain medication. And rarely does anyone turn down a drink, as they do more often in contemporary films. A poster used in the anti-smoking campaign in the public school system in Bremen, Germany, shows Humphrey Bogart and Ingrid Bergman standing with their backs together, with Ingrid thinking to herself, "Schade dass er raucht"—Too bad he smokes. The charm and sophistication of the smoker may have been considerable when the film *Casablanca* was made in 1942, but smoking has since lost much of its appeal, especially in romantic relationships. And "funny drunks" now seem to be far less common than they used to be. Being stupid, out of control and dangerous to others is no longer seen as worthy of laughter, at least by adults. Abusing alcohol is now more likely to be viewed as a social concern that affects the welfare of all of us, rather than something that only affects the drinker that the rest of us can laugh at. Moderation, if not abstinence, is more often expected of people today, although again not necessarily in the teenager's world of experimentation and rebellion.

Deciding not to drink does not necessarily mean that one will never, ever take a drink. A more reasonable and realistic definition of a nondrinker is that *as a rule they don't drink.* Absolute rules are more difficult to live by than flexible, more realistic ones that allow for occasional exceptions. For example, indulging on special occasions—having a glass of champagne to toast newlyweds, wine at Passover, "spiked" eggnog at Christmas or New Year's Eve—does not disqualify you as a nondrinker. As a general rule you might not eat red meat or french fries, but that doesn't mean that you never, ever do so. Sure, once in a while you find yourself in a situation when you have turkey and stuffing (with a bit of sausage or bacon in it), or a hamburger with a few fries. But these occasional dietary rule-bendings will not poison you. So by nondrinkers, we just mean that in the course of ordinary living, their habits do not normally include drinking alcoholic beverages.

It is also important to note that if you are a nondrinker, you should be tolerant of those who do drink, if you want to get along with the majority of people who are drinkers and avoid the risk of becoming unwanted company. You must realize that everyone has the right to decide what to do with their lives, just as you have chosen to be a nondrinker. No one likes having a critical, disapproving person around, and even subtle frowns are often interpreted as the mark of a social wet-blanket. It's one of the realities of social situations that to whatever extent you can participate in the mutual fun and social atmosphere, you will reduce the chances of becoming unwanted or regarded as a disapproving outsider.

HOW TO BE A NONDRINKER

There two sets of factors that tend to influence the uncommitted teenage drinker or nondrinker to drink. One is *social circumstances* that facilitate or encourage drinking, and the other is a *personal desire* or temptation to drink. You, as a parent, have to be aware of both influences if you are to help your teenager develop and then maintain an abstinent lifestyle. Social circumstances that would encourage teenagers to decide to drink include such situations as parents who drink a lot and model heavy drinking for their kids, or living in a neighborhood where teenage drinking is the norm, so that all kids—yours included—are pretty much expected to indulge as part of everyday life and growing up. The obvious remedies for influences such as these are to cut down on your own drinking and to move. Clearly this is easier said than done. Leaving the neighborhood is usually impractical and wherever you go there will still probably be *some* pro-drinking pressure. Let's look at some of the strategies young people can use to effectively resist the world of alcohol.

Dealing with social pressure to drink

As we have already stressed, teenagers are particularly susceptible to social pressure. Although social pressure to drink may not be as blatant as it used to be, teenagers' desire for acceptance makes them highly influenced by peer group expectations about drinking. In addition to all the cultural modeling and enticement to try the forbidden fruit, experience the novel, be independent, act like an adult, or rebel against adult authority, peer pressure exerts the strongest influence. If your teen has friends who drink, they will strongly influence the chances that your teen will also drink. More often than not, this will be the decisive factor. And if your teen's friends drink a lot or have gotten into trouble from drinking, the risk that your teen will follow in their footsteps is even greater. That is one reason it is so important to try to have an influence on who your teenager's friends are, even though you obviously can't choose them. You can, however, subtly encourage the "right" companions by suggesting they join you and your teen for special treats or by pointing out nice characteristics of those friends you think will be best for your teen. But even kids who do not have drinking friends will encounter many drinking opportunities. It is part of life in our culture that someone at some time is going to offer your son or daughter alcohol when you are not there to do anything about it. If your teenagers have openly discovered and dealt with alcohol and drinking issues within the family since they were 10 or 12 years old, chances are good that they will be equipped with the skills and knowledge to handle the situation successfully. If a negotiated decision not to drink has been reached in your family and your teens have had plenty of opportunity to assert their own opinions and make decisions for themselves, they will probably be able to resist opportunities to drink.

Saying no

"Just saying no" to anything means having *learned* to say no by doing it so often that you can do it comfortably without a great deal of thought just like driving becomes after years of experience. It also means declining in a way that others find acceptable. "No thanks, Mom, I don't want to go to the show with you and Dad. Jim is coming over to visit." "I just don't see it the way you do. I think it's up to me to decide if I'm going to go into the family business or not. I know you think I should, but I'm just not so sure it's right for me." Expressing differences of opinion many times in a respectful way is what youngsters need to practice in order to succeed in saying no to alcohol when the opportunity arises, as it almost surely will. For those who have no experience in saying no, the chances that they will be able to stand their ground are dubious.

Hot spots

It is important to avoid or know how to deal with "hot spots"—situations where drinking risks are greatest. You will be able to help your kids remain sober if you first find out where they are going, who they will be with, what they will be doing and whether adults will be present at a party. Ideally you should already have discussed with them how they will deal with practical problems like transportation and what to do if someone they are with starts drinking. We have emphasized the importance of having an agreement to pick them up if they unexpectedly find themselves having to rely on someone who is drinking to drive and how you will deal with their errors of judgment or mistakes in a constructive way. If you find out they are planning to be with teenagers who they think will be likely to drink, or they don't know enough about what they will be doing and with whom, you may want to deny permission to go and explain why. They should know enough details about their plans to answer the basic questions any responsible parent would need to know. Uncertainties can sometimes be dealt with by calling other parents. If your children have a good history of checking in with you, you can have them call you during the evening. But there is no substitute for helping them plan *in advance* for any circumstances that might affect their chances of remaining sober and making it home safely.

The primary teen hot spot is parties, but spontaneous gatherings with friends can also offer drinking opportunities. Teenagers will need to feel capable of choosing a soda over a beer or a shot, and still have fun. Not passing judgment on others, not moralizing, and not being a zealot for their choice will all make it easier to handle potential drinking situations and still remain a part of their circle of friends. The ways teenagers personally handle the situation, remain safe and help their friends are skills they must learn ahead of time.

As to helping their friends, teenagers should know what they can and can't do. They can provide a valuable service as "designated driver" *if* the others are cooperative, do not challenge their authority when driving (such as drinking in the car) and are not disruptive of the driver's concentration by blasting the car stereo or being too boisterous. Being a designated driver is emerging as a highly respected social role.

If teenagers have any questions about problems that arise, they should feel free to call their parents and ask what they should do. Teenagers shouldn't try to take on too much responsibility because a difficult situation can easily become worse and they may find themselves in over their heads. Being safe themselves is their first priority.

Assertiveness

Assertiveness is the key to success. For teens to be assertive as nondrinkers means being confident in their choice not to drink; having "reasons" they are prepared to give to account for why they choose not to drink; looking the drink-pushers straight in the eye while stating their choice firmly, without flinching; reiterating that choice to their friends as often as necessary to make their decision stick; not being defensive when receiving any flack they might get for being different; and not interpreting the negative or irritated remarks of others as personal rejection, but rather as disappointment that they are not sharing the experience and the risks of drinking. These are all part of the social skills needed to say no and stick to it.

Reasons teens can give for not drinking can be nearly anything that is genuine:

- "I don't like the taste."
- "I have to drive."
- "I can't drink for health reasons."
- "I have two alcoholics in my family — no way I'm going to take that risk."

They should know *not* to say things that put others down:

- "You guys are jerks for drinking."
- "I don't like people who drink."
- "Drinking is evil."
- "Alcohol is for losers."

Practical books on assertiveness are available in most bookstores and can be easily understood by parents or teens. Learning assertiveness through role-playing situations can be very helpful. Have a neutral observer give feedback. Or better yet, record your children on videotape in a role-playing situation and then observe the tape together and practice until they have mastered keeping eye contact, clear voice tone, serious facial expression and verbal fluency with the person playing the role of the drink-pusher. This can be a fun exercise for teens to act out with their friends, since most youngsters love to ham it up for on-screen performances. More important, it is a very effective method of learning assertiveness.

What is a friend?

Discussing what a friend is can be another way to aid teens in dealing with difficult drinking situations. Knowing who their real friends are is important. Chances are they have not carefully considered what makes someone a true friend. Many of their "friends" may just be acquaintances or companions, just as they are for many adults who loosely call people their "friends," even though a careful look would probably disqualify many of them. Friends care about you and are concerned about your welfare. They want you to be happy and don't want to subject you to risks or to put you through something unpleasant. Friends don't want you to do something you really don't want to do even though they might find it desirable if you did it. And friends can be talked to honestly and asked for support as a nondrinker.

Nondrinking activities

Another key to abstinence is having a lot of satisfying nondrinking activities. Teens, like adults, who have a host of other pleasurable activities to choose from are less likely to drink. All along parents can be helpful in making it possible or easy for them to participate in sports, music, scouts, hobbies, church activities, clubs, or any form of contact with other teenagers who are a positive influence.

Dealing with personal weaknesses

For those who have decided to abstain from alcohol, the major risk in teenage drinking, in addition to the desire for acceptance, is a personal weakness, temptation or vulnerability to alcohol. Teens who are unusually desperate for social approval, or who are high-strung or anxious, may find greater relief from stress through alcohol than do most others. It is also more difficult to abstain for those teenagers who are bored, have few friends, don't do very many things, have nothing in particular that strongly interests them, or who already drink and have decided to stop. Also at greater risk are those teenagers whose parents drink a lot and have (probably unwittingly) instilled in them an expectancy that they too will be a drinker, perhaps even a heavy drinker. If a parent becomes a model of sobriety it will be easier for a teen to do the same.

Personal factors like these may take prolonged effort to change, but it can be done. Parents *can* be more praiseworthy of their kids and help improve their self-esteem and self-confidence, thereby reducing their extreme craving for acceptance. Parents will have to do this rather consistently and for some period of time. High-strung or socially isolated teenagers can be helped to develop their social skills. Encourage them to engage in beneficial activities or experiences, defray their expenses, or help organize and plan group outings. More social interaction helps develop better social skills and reduces social anxiety and hence a potential reason to use alcohol. Activities that are expressive, like sports, music, or arts and crafts, are known to help reduce stress and anxiety and can be especially helpful. Anything that makes it easier for teens to develop friendships and cultivate alternative activities that compete with drinking reduces risks. Show an interest in their activities yourself by discussing with them what they are doing and how they feel about it. Participate in those activities that you too would enjoy. Having fun together is as good a deterrent as any to developing an interest in drinking.

Step 6

Teaching Sensible Drinking
(If Nondrinking Fails)

We have discussed the pros and cons of drinking and have encouraged a careful consideration of the issues for those who are not already drinkers. There are some excellent reasons not to drink at all, or at least not to drink regularly. Yet the fact is that about two-thirds of adults drink, so we can expect a similar percentage of those who are not yet adults to eventually become drinkers. Regardless of how someone has become a drinker, if they drink then they have an obligation to themselves and to others to do so in the safest possible way. The guidelines for sensible drinking presented in this chapter are not based on folklore, but on scientific research and clinical experience. All drinkers should use these guidelines, and parents should make sure their children understand them (our earlier book, *The Better Way to Drink*, gives a more detailed account).

KNOW THE BASIC FACTS ABOUT DRINKING

If you choose to drink it is especially important to learn the essential facts of how alcohol affects you body and behavior (see Step 2). You need to understand how alcohol affects your emotions, your physical abilities (most importantly your driving skills), your studies, your work, your social behavior and your sexual performance. Knowledge of these effects will help the responsible drinker minimize risks and maximize the more desirable effects of alcohol. You should also know how rapidly alcohol is metabolized (one drink per hour), how much alcohol is contained in different kinds of alcoholic beverages, what a "standard drink" is so you can accurately count your drinks and the blood alcohol (BA) level someone of your weight will reach after consuming one to four drinks.

BE AWARE OF YOUR DRINKING WHENEVER YOU DRINK

Plan how you will drink before the occasion arises and pay close attention to your plan so you can maximize the benefits and limit the risks. Many drinkers actually tune out their mood and feelings instead of enjoying the pleasant change that alcohol usually produces; if you are going to miss the benefits you might as well not drink. And if you are getting too high, you need to be attuned to that and do something about it before it gets out of hand.

DRINK SLOWLY

Sip, don't gulp, your drink. It takes about 20 to 30 minutes for the system to absorb the alcohol from one drink and for you to feel its full effects. Therefore, if you are drinking too fast, the first drink will only begin having an effect as you are finishing your second drink. If you catch yourself sipping your drink too frequently, deliberately set it down and leave it there for awhile. Get into the habit of tasting and savoring your drinks. If you enjoy the flavor, slow down and get more out of it.

EAT WHILE DRINKING

This will slow down absorption of the alcohol and keep you from getting too high too fast. Especially for inexperienced drinkers, it is important that their blood alcohol level rises slowly because if their BA rises too fast, they may start feeling nauseous and could vomit. Eating also gives you something to do with your hands so you are not constantly, and often unwittingly, sipping your drink.

ALTERNATE NONALCOHOLIC DRINKS WITH ALCOHOLIC ONES

Since doing something that results in pleasure encourages doing it again, alternate alcoholic and nonalcoholic drinks to slow down the process and keep from overdoing it. This will help you monitor how high you are getting so you can control your drinking better. Today most hosts and hostesses provide nonalcoholic drinks at social occasions and nobody will know what you are drinking.

KNOW YOUR LIMIT

Establish your personal BA limit below 55, and consult the tables at the back of the book to stay below your limit. The lower the BA you are satisfied with, the more sensitive your body will continue to be to the effects of alcohol. Should you drink too much or too often your body will become tolerant and without realizing it you may be raising your limit and drinking more just to experience the same effects you used to get with less alcohol.

AVOID DRINKING FOR MORE THAN ABOUT AN HOUR

The most positive feelings from drinking occur when you start sober and your blood alcohol gradually rises. Once your BA approaches 40 to 50, the positive feelings begin to change and instead of feeling even better, you will begin to experience the negative effects of alcohol. The law of diminishing returns applies to drinking. Since the body adapts to the effects, to feel any higher you would have to drink a lot more—and more is not going to make you feel better, just drunker. If you plan to drink for more than an hour, limit yourself to one drink per hour after the first hour, sip it, alternate nonalcoholic beverages with alcoholic ones and be sure to eat something if food is available.

DO NOT DRINK DAILY OR EVEN REGULARLY

If you drink frequently, your body will adapt to the effects and you will likely find yourself drinking more because of your developed tolerance. If you drink only occasionally your body will remain sensitive to the effects and one or two drinks will easily be plenty for you to feel good. To be able to "hold your liquor" is actually nothing to brag about. It means you have had a history of drinking too much too often and that your body has adapted to that amount of alcohol on a regular basis. It is much better to be a "lightweight" and thus highly sensitive to the effects. How much alcohol you can or should drink, though, is best measured by your BA, and not simply by number of drinks. For example, in 1 hour's time a 100-pound person after one drink and a 200-pound person after two drinks will have about the same BA.

DRINK ONLY TO ENHANCE

Drink only to enhance a good time and not to ward off stress or a personal problem. Instead of helping, alcohol usually keeps you from resolving the problem and can even make it worse. On the other hand, if you are in a relatively neutral or good mood and if you drink only occasionally, alcohol has the potential to enhance. In general, alcohol facilitates the expression of the mood you were in before you started drinking. So if you are angry when you mix up a stiff cocktail, you could become hostile and aggressive after you drink it. If you are feeling pretty good, you will most likely become more relaxed and pleasant after a drink or two.

IDENTIFY LIGHT AND HEAVY DRINKING SITUATIONS

You should be able to identify the people, places and events that are associated with sensible drinking for you, and those situations in which you need to be extra careful because you tend to drink too much. Sometimes drinking has an especially strong personal appeal, such as after a really successful day when you just feel like celebrating. That's a time to be careful. Or perhaps you have a tendency to overdo it when you are with a particular group of people. In such situations be prepared ahead of time with counter-strategies. Have a drink-limiting plan and stick to it. For example, if you have a tendency to get caught up in the excitement of Friday night TGIF parties and typically drink without realizing how much, decide beforehand how many drinks you will have, carefully count them as you get each one and stick to your decision to stop at your limit. Have a nonalcoholic beverage first or between drinks, practice your "drink refusal lines" so they are on your mind, and separate yourself frequently from your drink (dance, visit with people and leave your drink behind, or at least set it down so you are not holding it all the time). Consider arriving late and leaving early. Regardless of what you do , plan specifically how you will deal with your personal drinking "hot spots" and stick to the plan.

AVOID DOING ANYTHING THAT REQUIRES RESPONSIBILITY WHEN DRINKING

When you are feeling somewhat intoxicated, it is not the time for making school, work or personal decisions, placing important phone calls or, especially, driving. Reserve your drinking strictly for times when you are "off duty."

DEVELOP AND MAINTAIN NONDRINKING ACTIVITIES

Most drinkers have a number of things they can do that seem to serve a purpose similar to what drinking does for them. For example, if you drink to relax or to become playful, be sure you continue to relax and become playful in other ways as well. Keep drinking in its place by trying to find plenty of alternative activities. You don't want to become dependent on drinking to enjoy life. Routine drinking is easy to fall into because alcoholic beverages are readily available, relatively cheap and quick-acting, so you have to cultivate and maintain other important activities to prevent drinking from occupying a central position in your daily life.

MAINTAIN THE ABILITY TO DO THINGS WITHOUT ALCOHOL

Be sure you can continue to do everything you like to do without relying on alcohol. For example, work on your skills at socializing and engaging others without drinking. Practice if you need to. Do not let drinking become a necessary part of how you go about meeting your needs—social, recreational or emotional.

DEVELOP THE SKILLS OF ASSERTIVELY REFUSING DRINKS

Become skillful and comfortable with assertively refusing drinks in situations where you don't want one. Never let anyone push alcohol on you. If you have a problem refusing drinks or are subjected to a lot of pressure to drink for any reason, practice refusing out loud. If you can, get someone to play the role of pusher as realistically and aggressively as he can and then rehearse standing firm, maintaining good eye contact, leaning toward him and speaking in a loud and clear voice. Say something like, "No thanks, I don't want one" or "No more for me" or "Nope, I've had enough." Let the pusher increase the pressure on you, refusing to take no for an answer. Keep repeating your refusal like a broken record until he finally gives up. Another defense is to use "fogging" in which you look for the grain of truth in a critic's statement and agree with it, thereby disarming him. For example when they say, "You're not drinking! Don't tell me you're a health freak!" you say, "You're right, I am concerned about my health, so I don't drink." You have not agreed that you're a freak, but you have agreed that you're concerned about your health. Continued practice and rehearsal with friends and relatives helps a great deal when you get into a real situation. If you can, do it on videotape, watch your performance and observe your strengths and weak points.

SITUATIONAL EXAMPLES

Here are a couple of examples of situations in which using these guidelines can be helpful. Let's say you are going to a party where there will be plenty of alcohol. Before leaving home decide who is going to drive. Unless you plan to use public transportation or are taking a taxi, you should have a *designated driver* who assumes full responsibility for driving and will remain completely sober. Or perhaps you are being health-conscious, and assuming it's not too far, you might decide to walk. Even if you are not the designated driver, you should make a decision prior to leaving for the party about whether or not to drink. If you decide not to drink for any reason, feel good about it and rehearse your lines in your head so you are ready to graciously, but firmly, decline any alcohol that is offered to you. If you decide that you will drink, remain alert to be sure you are being served standard drinks so that you can accurately keep track of them. You already know to stay below the maximum number of drinks you can consume to stay below a BA of 55. (If you are a 150-pound person, you could have one or two drinks in the first hour and, ideally, no more, but if you do drink more, then you should limit it to one drink per hour.) Count your drinks as they are served and make a point of eating something while drinking if you can. Be aware that alcohol affects your decision-making capacity as well as your ability to stick to previous decisions. Perhaps you can start the evening with a nonalcoholic drink, or make your second drink nonalcoholic. After finishing your first drink there is often a natural tendency to have a second, so consciously slow down and wait at least 30 minutes before drinking another alcoholic beverage. Pay close attention to changes in your feelings and sensations so that you can consciously enjoy the benefits. Between sips set your drink down for a while. Dance or move around and socialize without your drink in hand. If the occasion turns out to be a negative one, if you are in a bad mood or are in the midst of dealing with a significant problem, don't drink. And, because of the tolerance factor, drink only if you have not had a drink for at least a couple of days. Presuming you follow these guidelines, you should return home feeling fine and have no negative after-effects.

Another very common situation in which you should make a conscious decision is whether to have an occasional drink before dinner, or whether you ought to have wine or beer with your meal. We say "occasional," since drinking everyday reduces your sensitivity and insidiously fosters escalating consumption. Take care of any necessary chores or responsible activities before drinking and relax *before* you sit down for the drink. Be sure that you are in a relatively good mood so the alcohol doesn't elicit bad feelings. Measure spirits in a shot glass, or pour 4 ounces of wine, so you know that you're drinking a standard drink and can keep count. While drinking, pay close attention to the effects of the alcohol. Don't let the "cocktail hour" last more than an hour and heed your maximum number of drinks to stay well below a BA of 55.

Drinking, like any other activity that involves risks, requires experience to know how to do it carefully and safely. These principles of sensible drinking are simple, easy to remember and take just a little thought and effort to carry out. They are well worth the energy expended and will allow those who drink to do so safely and function in harmony with the alcohol-accepting society in which we live.

There may be some parents of teens who choose to take the European approach and teach their children how to drink sensibly at home. The Jensens, who emigrated from Denmark eight years ago, expressed their amused bewilderment over American ways of drinking. "Why is it that Americans pretend their kids will not drink until they are 21 years old? At home we make no big thing of a drinking age." They explained that age is not emphasized as such a critical issue in Europe and that families rather than peers have a lot more to do with introducing teenagers to alcoholic beverages. Quite often teenagers are served beer, sometimes diluted with lemon-lime soda or ginger ale, or if the family drinks wine, the children may be served too, especially at meals. Smaller children are not usually offered drinks but teens, particularly older ones, often are. In Europe, whether teenagers drink is not the critical issue that it is in the United States. It is more important that young people join in socially with the family and behave themselves regardless of alcohol consumption. The Jensens believe that Europeans expect all people to behave themselves after drinking, so they are less concerned about the possibility of a teen "acting up" after drinking a glass of wine or two.

In all cultures maturing teens become more and more like their parents in adopting a variety of adult behaviors and attitudes. When it comes to drinking, the gradual developmental changes of teenagers are more naturally integrated over time in the European family and are not so age-dependent. The Jensens believe that as teenagers mature, they should be treated more and more like adults. Abrupt rule changes for behavior, such as overnight permission to drink at age 21, prevent learning about drinking under favorable conditions over time. They believe that it is the trial-and-error learning *outside the family* that is the cause of many of the problems Americans have with youthful drinking. The Jensens decided that in all fairness they had to give their children the benefit of their own experience with alcohol and opted to teach them to drink at home. Both of their teens were permitted occasional small amounts of beer and wine with dinner, beginning at about age 16. The Jensens are moderate drinkers, rarely have more than two or three drinks themselves, and thus are good role models for their children. And of course they are using some of the principles listed above by eating along with drinking, by drinking for less than an hour at a time, drinking slowly and drinking lightly, so their peak BA will always be quite low. Moreover, they drink only occasionally, generally with meals, to enhance an already pleasant time with their family and friends. Usually the Jensen's teens do not drink when their parents are drinking, and they do this with the knowledge that they could indulge if they chose. They are involved in many activities, do not rely on alcohol as a social lubricant and know how to comfortably refuse drinks they don't want. The Jensens are aware that their kids take an occasional drink when they are out with friends. They are concerned about the legalities of underage drinking and about drinking while driving, but trust their children to exercise good judgment, something they believe they have learned at home. The Jensens consider drinking to be in its proper place in their family—an issue but only a minor one.

Step 7

Dealing with Teenage Alcohol Abuse

Nineteen-year-old Tom lives comfortably at home with his parents who require him to pay $200 a month to cover his room and board expenses. He does virtually no household chores as his parents have never asked him to, and his job as a clerk in a local department store generates enough income to cover his car payments, allow him to eat out often, pay for entertainment and purchase a sixpack of beer after work each day. His habit is to come home at 5:30 and watch the news on television for a couple of hours while he drinks the sixpack. Depending on whether or not he likes what his mother is cooking for dinner, Tom eats at home or goes out. If he goes out, he often stops at a buddy's house for a couple more beers before having dinner. His parents worry about his excessive drinking and have tried to get him to cut down on his beer habit, but with little success. So far Tom's drinking has created no problems other than his parents' concern.

Susan is a 17-year-old senior in high school who is average in most respects. She gets along quite well with her parents, who have occasionally allowed her to drink wine with them at home. Susan has rarely done anything that displeased her parents, but during the previous six months she has come home drunk twice. She also had a drunk-driving conviction that resulted in a three-month driver's license suspension and a fine of $600, which her parents paid since she had no savings of her own. Each time she got drunk it was on a Saturday night when "partying" with the same group of friends. Each time this happened her parents were extremely distressed and pleaded with her to never do it again. Susan tearfully reassured them, with great remorse and sincerity, that she never would.

Fifteen-year-old Jerry is dismayed because he is a good 3 or 4 inches shorter than most of his buddies who have all experienced a significant adolescent growth spurt. He is unusually susceptible to social influence because of his size and need for acceptance and readily caves in to social pressure from his friends. He can successfully be dared to try almost anything and has even on occasion suffered serious physical consequences as a result, like the time he drank half a bottle of Tabasco sauce, or social embarrassment like the time he walked up to a total stranger in public and told her he'd like to have sex with her. This escapade provided great laughs for his buddies, but great embarrassment for the girl and regret for Jerry. Jerry actively dislikes the flavor of all alcoholic beverages but has managed, under pressure from his friends, to down a beer or two on a few occasions, each time resulting in a major problem. One time he jumped into his parents' car with several chums and went for a high-speed drive that got them stopped by the police. Another time, after just one beer, he became so boisterous that a couple of his "friends" roughed him up a little just to get him to shut up. On another drinking episode, after drinking some beer with his companions, they vandalized a neighbor's car with spray paint. Jerry had never committed any serious antisocial acts when sober, nor had he ever before had any altercations with his friends.

Which of these three teenagers is abusing alcohol? Tom, who drinks a sixpack of beer or more every night but has not gotten into any trouble for it? Susan, who rarely drinks but gets drunk when she does? Or Jerry, who has a history of rather serious antisocial behavior when he drinks even a small amount of beer?

The answer is that all three of them are alcohol abusers. Aside from being underage for drinking legally, which is a separate and important issue in itself, each of these teens abuses alcohol as measured by one or more of the three main criteria for determining abuse: *quantity* (judged by blood alcohol level), *frequency* (how often someone drinks) and *consequences*. Tom, the first example, weighs 160 pounds, so a sixpack of beer in 2 hours gives him a legally drunk BA of over 100. A BA of 55 is the upper limit for our definition of moderation, so Tom clearly consumes an excessive quantity of alcohol. He also drinks daily and thus too often, so he qualified as an abuser by this criterion as well. So far Tom has escaped any serious consequences resulting from his drinking, but that is probably just a matter of extremely good luck. If he keeps it up long enough, he will inevitably suffer some physical pathology, such as liver damage, and is likely to be arrested for drunk driving or some other drinking-related illegality. Susan also drinks too much, but she does not do it often. She clearly has a problem: she loves her parents, is terribly remorseful when she upsets them with her drinking and always promises them that she will not drink again—yet she does. As well, the legal consequences of her behavior under the influence also qualify her as an abuser. Jerry could not be judged an abuser by either the quantity or the frequency criterion, but his actions and the inevitable serious consequences after even light drinking make him an alcohol abuser.

So what specifically is alcohol abuse? For one thing, it is drinking to above a BA of 55. Changes in behavior and emotions are most significantly related to BA level. The higher the peak BA and the longer it is maintained, the more abusive the drinking. More than two drinks in an hour for an average-sized person would result in a BA above 55 and is therefore abusive. Drinking for longer than an hour, even with a BA below 55, progressively moves toward abuse. Two or even three hours of drinking with a BA well below 55 (say, 10 or 20) is not abusive, especially if it isn't done very often, but a BA of 55 or higher maintained for 2 hours or more is abusive.

Alcohol abuse also involves frequency of drinking. Drinking more than once every 2 or 3 days is potentially too often, depending on how high the BA reached is. For example, drinking every other day to a BA or 10 is not abusive either, but drinking once a week to a BA of 70 is abusive. This is precisely how teenagers often abuse alcohol—weekly episodes of excessive drinking. So too much alcohol and drinking too often are primary criteria for deciding whether drinking is abusive or not. The third factor is what happens as a result of drinking. Any amount of drinking that induces risky behavior, like driving after drinking, is abusive.

Teenage drinking is particularly hazardous in this regard. A major problem for teenage drinkers is that often they have not matured enough to have reliably good judgment even when sober; the added impairment to their judgment that alcohol causes only makes this worse. Also, being more active, energetic and daring than most adults, teenagers can easily fall prey to accidents. Other possible negative consequences for teenagers in particular include misbehavior after drinking, such as public drunkenness, disturbing the peace, or even vandalism. Delayed consequences include such things as declining grades in school, decreasing performance in sports or other activities, and a shrinking circle of friends that includes mainly other alcohol abusers.

In short, then, *alcohol abuse means drinking to a BA above 55, drinking more often than every couple of days, or doing risky or unacceptable things under the influence.* There are many degrees of abuse, from mild to extremely serious. Extreme abuse is often called "alcoholism" or, more recently, "alcohol dependence." Alcohol dependence is characterized by a very high tolerance to the effects of alcohol and a strong compulsion to drink. Drinking plays a central role in the dependent person's life and usually results in major damage to one or more areas such as personal relationships, job and health, as well as creating legal troubles.

While these definitions of alcohol abuse and dependence apply to all drinkers regardless of age, teenagers are a special case because legally they shouldn't be drinking at all. But the fact is they do drink. The seventh *Alcohol and Health* report to the U.S. Congress (1990) states that "92 percent of [high school] seniors in 1988 had tried alcohol, two-thirds were current drinkers, more than one-third were occasional heavy drinkers, and nearly one-third reported that most or all of their friends got drunk at least once a week." These statistics reflect the fact that the majority of teenagers drink by the time they are seniors in high school and that drinking is a problem, or potential problem, for many of them. When these teenagers have passive or unconcerned parents, dangers such as teenage drunk driving are far greater than if active parental efforts are made to help. When a parent ignores their child's drinking, or simply and ineffectually tells them not to do it, is irresponsible in our view, and *increases* the chances of both present and future trouble. Teenagers need guidance and if parents fail, which they sometimes do, it shouldn't be because they didn't try.

One thing that is important to know about teenage and young adult drinkers is that their drinking patterns usually tend to change markedly over time. Research shows that their manner of drinking at one point in life is very likely to be different a few years later. To quote once again from the seventh *Alcohol and Health* report: "During the transition years between adolescence and young adulthood there appears to be little continuity in drinking behavior, and drinking levels tend to decline substantially by age 30." Parents can take heart from this finding; in other words, it is not the end of the world if your teenager drinks or has a drinking problem now. However, as we have emphasized throughout this book, whether or not a teenager ultimately decides to be a nondrinker or develops safe drinking habits is, without a doubt, influenced by what you as parents do. If you are a responsible and involved parent, and if you make a concerted effort to help your children, persisting even the going gets tough, the odds are in your favor that they will finally emerge as sensible drinkers or nondrinkers. Don't expect immediate miracles and don't get discouraged and give up!

FOUR RISK FACTORS

Concerned parents can make good use of four known risk factors for alcohol abuse by teenagers: lack of parental monitoring; truancy and school failure; associating with deviant peers; and early, regular use of alcohol.

Parental monitoring

As we discussed in Step 3, Maximizing Parental Influence, knowing where your kids are, who they are with and what they are doing is knowledge that is critical to good parenting in general and especially important in preventing or dealing with drinking problems. Additionally, participating in their activities gives you more direct access to influencing them. It also makes you aware of who their friends are and which ones you want to encourage contact with. A close relationship, or at least one that gives you reliable information about them, will also tell you if there is a problem of almost any kind. You will be able to discuss their drinking directly with them by expressing your concern and offering your help. If there have been incidents in your family like the ones described at the beginning of this step, then you already have evidence to confront them with. If nothing blatant has yet occurred but you are suspicious, you may need to monitor them more carefully and do some investigative work. If your teens are reluctant to tell you their whereabouts and activities, insist that they do so or they will lose certain privileges that are precious to them (like driving or staying out late on weekends).

Unsupervised teenage parties are very risky, so adults should always be available. They don't necessarily have to be in the same room, just available nearby, and they should occasionally check up on things.

Blood alcohol measuring devices can be quite useful not only for detecting drinking, but also for measuring amount of consumption. Because of the high cost of such devices, in extreme cases where honesty is in question, an alternative is to use urine samples that can be professionally analyzed for alcohol and drugs, as will be discussed later in this chapter.

Truancy and school failure

If your kids are not doing well in school or are truant, you can and should do something about it. Perhaps the best book available to help with these adolescent problems is *Parents and Adolescents Living Together*, by M.S. Forgatch and G.R. Patterson (1989). Working with school counselors and authorities is also recommended. They will be only too glad to help, so call them and develop a joint effort between the family and the school.

Deviant peers

For practical reasons it can be difficult to influence a teen's friends and companions. It is not unusual for them or their parents to be unresponsive or even hostile to your concern, and they may accuse you of meddling in their private family business. If your teen is basically well-behaved and has not gotten into major trouble, but you have a hunch that peers or a particular friend may be encouraging alcohol abuse, focus your attention on your teen's interactions with the people or person who concerns you and find out what is going on. Getting directly in touch with the parents of your teen's friends is a good first step. Find out what they know and the level of their concern. They may even have specific information about the nature of you son's or daughter's drinking and simply didn't realize that you were not aware of it. On the other hand, don't be surprised if they seem less than helpful. They may assume that you are criticizing their parenting abilities.

Regular early use of alcohol

Those who start drinking at an earlier age and continue to do so on a regular basis are more likely to develop drinking problems. We know that as many as 50 percent of seventh graders, and even 10 percent of preteens, have tried alcohol. Detecting those who continue experimenting or drink regularly, and intervening before habits are established, is especially important.

INTERVENTION

What to do with abusing teenage drinkers depends largely on their age, the seriousness of their drinking problem, and the personality of the teenager. Also, how well they are doing in school and social relationships and their family values are important factors that influence the goal and the approach of an intervention plan.

Abstinence is the only acceptable goal in some families, regardless of the age of the teenager, and certainly it is the reasonable goal with younger teens. Abstinence for all teenagers is not feasible, though, given the social milieu in which most teens live or have to adapt to. Serious problems resulting from drinking usually imply stronger measures to change drinking behavior. Good personal adjustment augurs well for a more favorable outcome than less stringent intervention measures.

What we are going to suggest for dealing with teenage alcohol abuse requires forethought and skill on your part, so prepare carefully. In planning your approach, talk it over carefully with your spouse so that the two of you can present a united front. And be realistic in your plans. Since an older teenager cannot be monitored 24 hours a day and is growing increasingly independent in decision-making and behavior, don't try to impose rules you cannot enforce.

If your teenager has only experimented with alcohol and nothing really bad has happened as a result of their experimentation, perhaps the safest and best thing to do is to try to influence him not to drink at all. (The steps on Influencing Decisions About Drinking and Helping Teens Abstain will be useful to reread for ideas about reasons not to drink and ways to strengthen your teenager's ability to abstain.) Since most teens normally have some degree of conflict with authority, involving them in a discussion of the reasons for not drinking and getting their input on how they feel about it and what they think might work, usually will improve the chance of success. Sometimes a reasonable discussion and a joint decision not to drink works, especially with more compliant teens. But it is important to monitor them to be sure of any changes in their disposition.

Alcohol-abusing teenagers who are unreasonable or not very compliant will need a stronger approach to change their drinking behavior, especially if abstinence is the goal. Scare tactics may help at times, but only if the evidence for the point being made is true. If your children find out that what you are telling them is not true, you lose your credibility and it might cause them to try out whatever you say is bad (because in *their* experience what you say is bad is really good). Among examples of the misuse of scare tactics were the films shown in high school classes back in the '50s that featured advanced cases of venereal disease replete with black, shriveled-up, disfigured genitals. Teenagers were warned that this would be their fate if they had sex. These films fostered a fear of sex, but not avoidance of it. Eventually teenagers found out that with normal precautions such terrible consequences would not occur, and they resented being purposely manipulated and traumatized by adults.

In some instances the emotional impact of walking through the seamy side of town to see winos sprawled out on the sidewalk, exposed to the elements; a ride with the police for the same purpose, which can be arranged in some communities; a visit to the drunk tank at the city jail or a trip to the alcohol ward at a hospital can help strengthen the conviction of some youngsters to refrain from drinking or to be more careful about using alcohol. Just be sure that what they see and hear is portrayed truthfully as genuine problems resulting from long-term alcohol abuse, and not some fable made up to portray the universal effects of "demon rum." It is reasonable to assume that teenagers already know that the majority of drinkers are not like this and drink without experiencing serious consequences.

When parents are not sure whether they can believe their teens, they may be able to get help from modern medical technology. Other then owning a breath analysis device, which is expensive, one simple way to get direct, objective evidence of drinking by a teenager is to obtain a urine sample for alcohol and drug testing. Tamper-proof containers for urine collection are available from many medical laboratories and some doctors' offices. An analysis for alcohol and drugs usually costs about $20 to $30. Discuss the drinking rules with your teens and tell them that you will be obtaining a urine sample when they return home. Collect the sample in a matter-of-fact way and store it in the refrigerator. Make sure the sample they give you is warm so you know it has just been supplied and is theirs. There is no reason to discuss anything at the time you obtain the sample, thus eliminating a conflict over any questions about drinking. From the results of the analysis you will know if your teen was drinking and, if so, the approximate BA level.

Overt evidence of alcohol abuse, or from breath or urine samples that show high BA levels, indicates the need for powerful and active intervention by parents. Let's assume you have evidence of abusive drinking by your teenage son and are going to confront him with it. The confrontation itself should be done at a formal family meeting when he is sober. Certain ground rules must apply, such as only one person speaking at a time, no shouting or tone of disrespect, and no interruptions. While everyone gets a chance to speak, repeated violations of the ground rules will terminate the meeting (termination means indefinite suspension of privileges until a new meeting resolves the issue).

Be direct in conveying your observations or other knowledge of his drinking. Say that until everything is worked out he cannot use the car, stay out late, go to the mall (or lose other significant privileges important to him), and that for now he must come home right after school. Adjust the period of loss of privileges according to the seriousness of the infraction. For example, if he drove home after drinking, you could suspend driving privileges for a couple of weeks because this is a serious rule violation. If he came home in a responsible manner after drinking too much (didn't drive and rode with a sober driver), perhaps the suspension should be just a single week. If he does not drive, then restrictions on telephone or social privileges may be used. In addition, tasks like cleaning up their rooms, mopping floors, cleaning out the garage, or pulling weeds are all suitable penalties allowing teens to work their way back into good family standing. Let the punishment fit the crime and be matter-of-fact about it (don't lecture, scold or nag). Be specific about when privileges will be restored, and under what conditions.

With this plan you can discourage drinking that produces overt signs, at least the ones you can monitor. Realistically, though, they still may drink when outside your supervision. If they do drink, at least they will have to do it with considerable caution and control or they risk getting caught and paying an even higher price the next time. A second offense should be known to result in more severe consequences.

Let's use 17-year-old Susan, the high school senior we described at the beginning of this step, as an example of implementing a plan to change a teenager's drinking behavior. She apparently does not drink very often, but when she does, it is very excessive. Her remorseful promises to quit have not been kept, so her parents have decided to do something more than make another heart-wrenching plea to stop drinking. The last time she was found to be drinking they had a serious discussion with her in which they made it clear that the next time she drank there would be specific consequences involving loss of driving, telephoning and socializing privileges. Susan agreed to the plan but didn't feel it was necessary since this time she really would stop drinking with her friends. The following dialogue took place on a Sunday morning after she came home drunk once again.

Mom:	You came home drunk again last night and we want to talk to you about it. The rules for this discussion are that we won't interrupt each other or say unkind things, and will hear each other out. It is to your advantage to listen to what we have to say because you won't be able to drive or make phone calls, and must return home from school within one hour, until these restrictions are lifted. Do you understand?
Susan:	(a bit shocked and confused) You mean I can't drive the car or make *any* phone calls?
Dad:	That's right. We have decided that to help you get control of your drinking we must do something more than just talk about it. You can earn your privileges back, but only by staying sober, just as we discussed the last time this happened.
Susan:	But I wasn't driving last night. Jim was, and he only had a couple of drinks.
Mom:	Susan, you came home really drunk again, after telling us it would never happen again. This time you will lose the use of the car and the telephone, as we agreed to last time. And you must come home within one hour after school is out. Assuming you stay sober, in one week you can start using the phone again, in two weeks, you won't have to come

	home from school right away, and after three weeks your car privileges will be restored.
Susan:	That's ridiculous! You're crazy if you think you can keep me from driving my own car! I don't care what you say…
Dad:	(interrupting Susan's loud voice) The rule is no raised voices. You won't be driving anyone's car or using the phone until you earn these privileges back. And keep a civil tone in your voice. Do you understand?
Susan:	(surprised at her parents' unusually stern reaction, and somewhat subdued) I guess so…
Mom:	How did this happen again?
Susan:	(after a long pause) Well, we were all over at Linda's house. We were just having fun. And I had some drinks. (another long pause)
Mom:	You must have had a lot of alcohol to come home in the shape you were in last night. We don't need to hear the details just now, unless you want to tell us more. (pause, no response) OK. As I said, for staying sober for one week you will earn back the use of the phone, in two weeks you don't have to come home right after school, and in three weeks you can drive again. If you want to clean up your room and and do a thorough job of it, we will cut the coming home from school penalty to just one week. Ten hours of yard work will get your car back a week earlier. To *keep* phone use and driving privileges, though, you will have to *stay* sober. And if there is any evidence of your drinking — coming home smelling of alcohol, any beer cans or bottles of liquor anywhere, or anything else suggesting any drinking — you will lose these privileges again and will have additional penalties. Do you understand?
Susan:	Yes.

There is, of course, no guarantee that this plan will be effective. If your teen does drink again, you must follow through with the promised penalties, stick to your guns, and maintain a firm position in order to maximize the chances of success in the long run.

DEALING WITH LEGAL AND SOCIAL PUNISHMENT

Should your teen's drinking result in some kind of punishment other than what you have specified, it is generally best not to intervene, and especially not to come to the rescue. You may be sympathetic about you teen's chastisement by school or police, but real-life consequences like being locked up overnight can have a major inhibiting effect on abuse of alcohol in the future *if you don't rescue him*. Parents are not the only ones who are concerned about teenage alcohol abuse. In fact, other authorities may have an even greater impact. Imagine a 17 year old, for example, experiencing the shock and humiliation of prisoner treatment and locked detention in juvenile hall as a consequence of drinking (those over 18 are considered adults and go to jail instead of juvenile hall). It could be just the ticket to discourage future alcohol abuse. You should remain fairly neutral, or maybe a little sympathetic, but it could be a great mistake to take the sting out of the punishment. It is usually therapeutic to just let arrested teens stew in custody for a time, despite pleas to get them out. For example, if the police call you at 2:00 in the morning to say they have picked up your son for a drinking-related offense and you can come and get him at any time, don't be in any rush to do so. Unless he has never drunk before to your knowledge, and there has never been a drinking problem of any kind, let him spend the night, or even longer if his drinking has been a serious problem for some time. Require him to use his own funds to pay bail or any fines, or at least exhaust whatever funds he does have. This way the effect of societal intervention on his drinking will be maximal.

It is more loving to restrain yourself from doing what makes you feel better at the moment than it is to rescue your kids immediately. Instant rescue may be indulging your personal need to feel like a "good parent," but it is at their ultimate expense. In this difficult situation created by their drinking, try to understand your own motivation if you feel a compelling urge to come to the rescue. Whose needs are being met? Who is dependent on whom? Is your life made more meaningful through solving your kids' problems for them rather than letting them grow up? What will be the long-term consequences for them if you do get them off? Overprotecting your children keeps them from learning about the reality of alcohol abuse, and prevents them from changing their ways. They learn to simply let you get them out of trouble rather than avoiding trouble in the first place.

TEACHING SENSIBLE DRINKING AS AN ALTERNATIVE APPROACH

Setting consequences for abusive drinking by your teenager as just described is one way of dealing with the problem. Another approach is to attempt to teach teens to drink responsibly. Recognizing their growing independence, your decreasing influence on them, and the likelihood that they may soon be moving out of your home anyway, you might wish to try teaching sensible drinking patterns at home under your supervision, making you an ally rather than an enemy, in dealing with a troublesome problem. You would specify the conditions under which they would learn to drink responsibly. This might include drinking only when you are present, no drinking with friends, and no indications that they are drinking at other times (no beer cans, wine bottles or liquor containers full or empty, no coming home smelling of alcohol, and no hanging out with kids who drink abusively). You could insist that they never ride with anyone who has been drinking. Instead, they should call a taxi (which you would pay for), ride with someone who is totally sober, or call you for a ride at any time of the day or night, as suggested by SADD'S Contract for Life.

If you are going to attempt to teach your teenagers moderate drinking, spell out the plan carefully. They must learn to sip their drink slowly and really taste it. Most important, they must pay attention to the effects so they learn to monitor their sense of intoxication. They should do this only in your company under positive conditions such as just before or during dinner. Obviously, no chugging and no drinking games would occur as might happen when drinking with other teenagers. Have them carefully monitor the number of drinks and limit that number so that their BA would be well below 55 (less than two full drinks for someone weighing about 120 pounds). A plan for teaching teens about sensible drinking should only be used when you are present to observe and control the situation. Should they violate the rules of the plan, such as by drinking at other times, you can enforce them with consequences such as those discussed earlier. Drinking moderately and safely, as described in Step 6, Teaching Sensible Drinking, can serve as a guide for these efforts. Our earlier book, *The Better Way to Drink*, gives even more detailed and useful information on how to drink responsibly.

One reminder: Teens are more responsive to parents who only try to influence them about a *few* major issues. Fighting them across the board on many of their behaviors that you don't like is almost sure to fail, and will probably make your relationship with them a constant hassle. So carefully select your priorities. It is not important, and virtually impossible and undesirable anyway, to have kids do everything exactly as you want them to. Absolute control over your children is not the issue. Helping them grow up to be responsible adults is the concern, and alcohol is one of the important things they need to learn to deal with as part of the maturation process.

GETTING OUTSIDE HELP

For parents who find themselves overwhelmed and simply unable to be effective in dealing with their children's drinking, professional therapy or other outside help might be useful. Churches often provide counseling at little or no cost, and high school counselors can sometimes make referrals to specific community agencies or specialists. The county mental health department and college counseling centers also make referrals. Alcoholics Anonymous (AA), Rational Recovery (RR), Secular Organizations for Sobriety (SOS), and other alcohol abuse treatment programs, many of which have adolescent groups or are designed specifically for young people, are listed in the yellow pages of your telephone book under mental health services. Psychologists or psychiatrists may provide services or give information that may lead to help. In more extreme cases of alcohol abuse or when parents have lost control and need some relief, an inpatient hospital program for adolescent alcohol abuse may be appropriate. In such cases a short-term stay of about two weeks can sometimes initiate changes, but those changes must be maintained by the family. Therefore, hospital programs that involve the parents in the treatment process, and help them plan for the continuation of the therapeutic program after discharge, have a better chance of success. So find out about the specifics of any inpatient program you are considering. When calling for information about any kind of treatment or professional services, describe your teenager's behavior ("she has come home drunk several times and has been missing school") rather than offering a label ("she's an alcoholic"). To a referring person or health professional, specific but brief descriptions of the essence of the problem are more useful than an unconfirmed, general label. It will take a bit of telephoning and investigative work to follow through on leads for professional assistance, but persistence will pay off.

A word of caution: there may be many "professionals" who will claim to be able to help, but the degree of help may vary considerably. Your task is to find out which professionals in your area have the best reputation for treating exactly the kind of problem facing you and your child. When the same name keeps coming up from different sources, you may be on to the right person. In our opinion, professionals who want to see the parents and teenager together, rather than the teen alone (at least at the start of therapy) will deal with the problem more appropriately. We see teenage alcohol abuse as a problem that is best dealt with in the context of the whole family. Also, experienced professionals with a social learning or behavioral approach are often more successful in these cases. But individuals from any orientation or professional background with a good reputation for dealing specifically with teenage alcohol abuse can certainly be as effective.

CHECKLIST OF STEPS TO HELPING YOUR TEEN

1. Is your teen drinking?

2. If so, under what circumstances and what problems has it caused?

3. To what extent would your teen's drinking be judged abusive?

4. Have you considered the four risk factors to reduce problems with alcohol (lack of parental involvement, truancy and school failure, deviant peers and regular, early use of alcohol)?

5. If you need to intervene, have you taken into account their age, the reality of their social situation, the nature and seriousness of their drinking, and the level of their personal maturity and adjustment?

6. Have you made a plan with your spouse that you both agree on and are able to enforce?

7. Do you know how to utilize the punitive consequences resulting from their drinking that have been imposed by legal or other authorities?

8. Have you considered teaching sensible drinking skills to older teens?

9. Have you thought about outside help if necessary?

Teenage alcohol abuse is a common problem that affects thousands of families, so if it happens to your family, rest assured that you are not alone in suffering the resultant emotional pain and distress. The fact that you are trying to do something about the problem makes your commitment to being a responsible parent clear, and you should feel good about the effort.

PART 3

Preventing Problems

With any serious public health problem the most effective course of action is to prevent the problem from developing in the first place. This approach has virtually eliminated smallpox, polio, and even death by lightning (using the simple preventive measure of installing lightning rods to ground buildings). Prevention of alcohol abuse is also possible, and the last two steps of the overall program focus on preventing drinking problems by helping preteens understand and prepare for drinking issues and decisions, and on fostering improvements in the way society regards alcohol. We are learning more about factors that increase the chance of trouble with alcohol and how to use that information to intervene early or to prevent the problem from developing altogether. The emphasis on prevention will require working more effectively with preteens as well as teenagers, and making some important societal changes in our assumptions and beliefs about the use of alcoholic beverages.

Step 8

Preparing Preteens

This step focuses on helping children who are 9 to 12 years old make better sense out of what they already know or are learning about drinking. It also lays the groundwork for establishing a basic understanding of the nature of alcohol use as a means of preventing children from ever developing a drinking problem. One advantage of starting with preteens is that they still tend to listen to their parents and are less influenced by their peers.

The 9 to 12 age group is ideal for beginning to understand the importance of alcohol in people's lives. In this age range children have already been exposed extensively to alcohol and drinking among adults on TV, in movies and at home. They are capable of developing a meaningful sense of family values and beliefs about drinking and alcohol, and even gaining an initial grasp of the role of alcohol in society at large.

To help your children you need first to clarify for yourself what your own values, beliefs and rules about drinking are. To answer your kids' questions and communicate effectively with them, you should be clear in your own mind whether or not you believe that drinking in moderation by you or by others is acceptable. If so, why? If not, why not? If you think total abstinence is best, be prepared to explain why you believe this to be the case. The facts about alcohol presented in Step 2, the pros and cons of drinking discussed in Step 4, and the guidelines for sensible drinking in Step 6 may be helpful in clarifying these issues.

It is also important that you are straightforward and honest with your kids. You have to establish credibility so they will trust you and know that they can come to you with questions and concerns about drinking in the future. So always tell them the truth, but gear it to their developmental level of curiosity and ability to understand. The importance of meeting kids at their current developmental level is well illustrated by 6-year-old Johnny who came to his mother one day and asked, "Mom, where did I come from?" Judging from the serious, quizzical look on Johnny's face, she assumed this was it; he was finally asking about the birds and the bees. Taking a deep breath to control her own discomfort about what she felt compelled to say, she launched into an elaborate account about how Johnny's father and she loved each other very much, and how they made love in a special way so that his seed was planted in her body. After several minutes of restless listening and a brief pause in mom's far too elaborate account, Johnny replied, "Well, I just wondered, because Jimmy down the block said he came from Chicago."

What kids know about alcohol may not be very accurate or even very clear in their own minds. The likely sources of their information are what they have seen on TV and in movies, perhaps some real-life observations of people drinking, and what other kids have told them, and maybe some kind of early alcohol education at school.

Begin by finding out what your child already knows about alcohol so you can correct his errors and build on his knowledge. Don't try to find out everything at once. Do it in brief "learning moments" that arise spontaneously or seem natural in the situation. For instance, you can raise questions about alcohol after a beer commercial that runs on TV, after seeing some character drinking in a movie, following your hosting a gathering of people who were drinking, or when you yourself are having a drink. The children may raise questions on their own. Their ideas will probably be pretty vague, so help them clarify their notions by rephrasing them as clearly as you can and seeing if you both agree on the point or question. Below are listed what we consider the ten basic questions that need to be discussed with preteens. This is a beginning, not an exhaustive list. Let children run with these issues and go wherever their curiosity leads.

1. WHY DO GROWNUPS DRINK?

This is one of the most common questions raised by young children. An honest and fairly simple answer is that most people drink because it relaxes them and makes them feel a little better, and they like the taste of alcoholic beverages. They usually feel more playful, friendly and talkative. Kids should also know that drinking does *not* make grownups feel great, and that they can't think or do things as well after drinking. Expectancies about the effects of alcohol should be accurate in terms of the positive effects as well as in terms of the limitations and impairments alcohol imposes on the drinker.

2. HOW COME SOME PEOPLE AREN'T NICE WHEN THEY DRINK?

First clarify the question. For instance, "Are you thinking of somebody in particular?" Or, "What have you noticed, what are they like?" Before you react, listen carefully to what they have to say and get the details about what they have observed and how they interpret it. It's OK to ask who they have in mind so that you can be specific in replying. Then use this opportunity to discuss their observations in the context of what too much alcohol does to people. For example, you might say that adults who drink a lot may become unpredictable and can be a problem because they are hard to talk to and don't think right. They can easily lose their balance and make mistakes like spilling things. The way adults feel when they have had too much to drink is dizzy, sleepy, tearful and silly; sometimes they get angry and upset. They might not be fun to be around and can be mean and nasty. Heavy drinkers can be dangerous to others, especially when they drive after drinking, because they can't see as well, they can't act quickly if they have to put the brakes on fast, and they can't make reliable decisions behind the wheel.

    If your child is talking about your own drinking, try not to get defensive. It could be that your drinking is perfectly normal but the child feels that *any* drinking is bad, or simply fails to understand the idea of acceptable drinking.

3.   DO YOU THINK DRINKING IS WRONG?

This question will give you a chance to explain your thoughts about drinking. It can be a chance to explain what sensible drinking is and why you drink, or why you choose not to drink. Use this as a teaching opportunity for you and a learning opportunity for them. Be aware that the main influence on a child's conception of drinking may very well be what you are like when you drink. You can tell them that you like to have an occasional drink or two when you are with certain friends, or at a barbecue, or after mowing the lawn, because it relaxes you, makes socializing more fun, tastes good, helps your to tune out of thinking about work for a while, or whatever else seems true to you.

It is possible that you become less accessible to your children when you drink and they don't like it. Ask them how they see you when you drink. Again, though, be prepared to help them clarify their response, and try not to be defensive about it. Maybe you do drink too much and need to consider doing something about it. In any case, a simple description of what moderate drinking is can give them some idea of what is acceptable. Essentially, moderate drinking is having a couple of drinks (or a bit more depending on body size) two or three times a week when you are off duty and having fun.

4.   WHEN IS DRINKING OK?

Children often want to know in which situations it is OK for adults to drink. A simple and plain answer might include drinking just before or with dinner, when friends visit, on a picnic, or at celebrations like weddings or certain religious ceremonies. When is it *not* OK? Before driving, mowing the lawn, working with power tools, when engaging in serious business of any kind, when doing anything even slightly risky, like standing on a ladder to paint, or when you are in a bad mood, because alcohol tends to exaggerate whatever mood you are in.

5. IF IT FEELS GOOD TO DRINK, THEN WHY DON'T PEOPLE DO IT ALL THE TIME?

Some people do drink practically all the time. These are the problem drinkers and we call them alcoholics. They tend to get into lots of trouble because you can't drink all the time and still get along in the world. But your kids have probably observed that most people who drink do it sensibly and in moderation, quitting after a couple of drinks. Kids can understand that anything that feels good can be overdone and cause problems. You can eat so much ice cream that you become sick, play so much outdoors that you don't do your homework, watch so much TV that there is no time to play with your friends, (or work so much you have no time to spend with your kids). The same thing is true of alcohol. If you drink too much alcohol you will feel worse rather than better. Too much drinking is especially problematic because it can limit or even destroy the ability to think straight and do things right.

6. WHY CAN'T KIDS DRINK?

An understandable question kids wonder about is how come alcohol is OK for adults but bad for kids. Tell them that children shouldn't drink because their bodies are growing and developing and that alcohol will interfere with their potential to become as healthy and smart as they can be. Their bodies are so much smaller compared with yours that even one drink can make them sick or drunk. Because they have no experience with the effects of drinking, they are more likely than most adults to take dangerous risks like riding a bike and being seriously hurt. Drinking threatens their ability to think and do their schoolwork. They need to develop more mature judgment to be able to know whether alcohol is all right for them, and that means waiting until they are older. For now, though, they should not drink. If they have a great curiosity about the taste of alcohol, and if it is compatible with your own values and family traditions about drinking, you might be better off to give them a sip to satisfy their curiosity (a taste of scotch whiskey is usually sufficient to thoroughly dampen most childhood curiosity). Denying them even a taste may enhance the mystery, increase the value of the "forbidden fruit," and in the long run create even more problems. It is better that they learn from you than from anyone else.

7. HAVE YOU EVER BEEN DRUNK?

Kids hear about drunk drivers, see people acting drunk in movies and on TV, and are curious about this strange phenomenon that has no parallel in childhood. If you have been drunk, tell them what it was like, how you felt, how it happened, and what came of the episode. They can understand being so dizzy they have trouble standing up, or feeling funny in the head and having difficulty thinking straight, or feeling sick to the stomach and perhaps throwing up. If you have never been drunk before, you have probably heard a good unsavory story to tell them about someone who has been. Be careful not to glorify the experience, as people sometimes do. Focus on the negative.

8. WHAT IS A HANGOVER?

As most kids have heard about being drunk, they will probably also have heard of hangovers. They can be told that when people drink too much they pay a high price physically—sort of like having the flu for a day. Excessive drinking has a big impact on the human body and puts it temporarily out of commission. It may take a day to recover. During that time, the drinker does not feel well, usually with a severe headache and upset stomach.

9. WHAT'S THE DIFFERENCE BETWEEN BEER, WINE, AND WHISKEY?

There are many variations on this theme—whiskey versus wine, beer versus ale, and so on. Tell them that there are many ways to produce the kind of alcohol that people drink. (Only one kind of alcohol is safe to drink—other alcohols like rubbing alcohol are poisonous.) Different alcoholic beverages can be made from different kinds of ingredients, such as grains like rice, wheat and barley, or fruits like grapes, pineapples and berries. Mixing these ingredients with water and letting them age (ferment), produces alcohol with the particular flavor of the ingredients used. And just as with various ice cream flavors, people usually have a preference for the type of drink they like. The amount of the alcohol in a particular alcoholic beverage depends upon how the fermentation process was carried out. Most beer, for example, is processed quickly and has much less alcohol than whiskey which ferments for years. Most teens can understand that a small glass of whiskey has the same total amount of alcohol in it as a large glass of beer. Beer is simply much more diluted.

10. WHAT SHOULD I DO IF SOMEONE OFFERS ME A DRINK?

Preteens are not very likely to bring this up directly, but it may appear in a question like, "Joey's father sometimes gives him a little glass of beer with dinner. Can I have one too?" Most families will have a strict rule that no drinking is allowed for preteens, and it is helpful to respond with specific instructions on how those rules should be implemented in various situations. They can, for example, be rehearsed to say, "No thank you, my family rule is that I can't drink any alcohol at all." They should be encouraged to report any such incidents to you—and be praised for doing so. They should understand that other families may have very different rules about drinking alcohol, but that your rules apply to your children no matter whose house they are in.

THE IMPORTANCE OF TIMING

Ask your preteens to come to you with anything involving alcohol. And when they do, invest a moment or two to take advantage of the opportunity to help them learn by responding thoughtfully. The best time to teach children is when *they* want to learn. Even if it may be a bit inconvenient, you will get through to them much better at the moment they ask a question or make a comment about alcohol. So even if their question is untimely, or perhaps fraught with concern because something upsetting has happened, such as someone offering them a drink, it is important to respond at the moment. Be gentle and helpful. Control your emotions and thank them for coming to you with questions about alcohol.

Depending on your own children's maturity or curiosity, there is something else that is important to tell them time and again, though it may not seem essential at this age. Drinking is *not* an excuse to misbehave or to do things other people don't like. Regardless of how much people might drink, if they do something unpleasant or dangerous to others, they are responsible for their behavior and should pay the consequences. It is especially not OK to drive after having more than a drink or two.

Step 9

Alcohol and a Changing Society

Overall, things are changing for the better in the way society looks at alcohol. Some of these changes have practical legal ramifications, such as the treatment of drunk drivers; others involve theoretical and technical medical developments, which will lead to an expansion of efforts aimed at prevention and early intervention in alcohol problems. Also changing are portrayals of drinking in the media and the promotion and sale of alcoholic beverages.

PREVENTION OF PROBLEMS

It was only a decade ago that most people working with alcohol abuse took the approach that there are only two kinds of drinkers: alcoholics and everybody else. Such all-or-none thinking is appealing because at first glance it seems to simplify the issue. Just arrive at a single a single judgment: either the person is an alcoholic or he is not. However, the problem is that in general people rarely fit easily into one of any two groups (except perhaps being anatomically male or female). As a result of this simple division, most drinkers thought they didn't have to pay much attention to their drinking because they assumed they weren't alcoholics. And since there was little agreement anyway on exactly what an alcoholic was, problem drinkers could easily dodge the facts of their abusive habits until some sort of disaster occurred. Over the years we have spent endless time, effort and money trying mightily to identify and treat the most severe abusers, or "alcoholics." At the same time we have given little consideration to the majority of drinkers, the so-called non-alcoholics, many of whom also drink too much. We now know that every drinker is at some risk of drinking abusively, not just those born with an unfortunate alcoholic genetic quirk or those who grew up tormented by alcoholic family hassles. All drinkers are at risk because drinking has pleasurable effects (for the vast majority) that encourage additional drinking, and any regular use of alcohol produces tolerance that can result in gradually escalating consumption. There are some individuals who for genetic, social or psychological reasons are at greater risk of developing abusive drinking habits than is the average drinker. Clearly, this group needs to be identified and warned of their increased risk. But these individuals are only a small proportion of the general population of drinkers. Genetic researchers have emphasized that repeated media reports have done the public a disservice by implying that alcohol abuse and dependence are primarily genetically transmitted, thereby offering a simple explanation for a complex biological-psychological-sociological problem. Many excessive drinkers do not view their overdrinking as anything like that of the alcoholic. Combined with the absence of evidence of genetically transmitted family alcohol problems, these drinkers often make little, if any, effort to cut back on their drinking. Today we regard them as alcohol abusers and we know how to help them. All of this underscores the fact that an effective preventive approach must target everyone at risk, which means *all* drinkers (a "primary prevention" model). This approach utilizes demonstrably effective public health procedures and makes infinitely more sense than spending the major portion of our energy and funds attempting to treat the most severe and chronic alcohol problems.

A new plan is emerging that considers the whole range of drinkers. We are pleased to note that the recent special report to Congress from the Secretary of Health and Human Services, *Alcohol and Health* (January 1990), has clearly moved in the direction long advocated by social-learning alcohol researchers. It recognizes that we can most sensibly view drinking in the same way we look at most other human behavior, occurring as a continuum, with nondrinkers at one end, alcohol-dependent drinkers at the other end, and various degrees of use and abuse in between. This approach logically encourages society to consider as its first and foremost priority facilitating more responsible choices about alcohol so that those who choose to drink can do so in the least risky way, perhaps preventing future problems altogether. It suggests that *all* drinkers need to monitor their drinking for early indications of undesirable drinking habits that could signal a growing health risk. Research on the development of tolerance to the effects of alcohol makes it clear that every drinker is at risk of drinking abusively over time, and that it is important to prevent tolerance from developing in order to prevent drinking problems. The contemporary view mandates devising effective methods for intervening in drinking problems early in their development rather than five, ten or twenty years later when there is less chance of major change. Current views of alcohol abuse also require specific treatment programs to meet the needs and backgrounds of specific individuals rather than assume that one treatment goal and one treatment method are appropriate for everyone. Similarly, matching types of abusive drinkers to specific treatment methods is another trend strongly encouraged by the federal government in its 1990 report, *Alcohol and Health.*

DRINKING AND DRIVING

Most people are now aware of the major worldwide shift in public attitude and criminal laws concerning driving while intoxicated (DWI), driving under the influence (DUI), or simply drunk driving (DD). Drinking and driving is a very serious issue today, a far cry from the "funny-drunk" jokes of earlier decades, the snockered humorous characters careening about in films and on TV, and the winking and giggling that occurred when individuals who could barely walk felt it was OK to get behind the wheel. We currently live in a get-tough-on-drunk-drivers society that is fed up with burying innocent people who died simply because alcohol interfered with someone else's coordination, vision and judgment. The term "designated driver" was rarely heard a decade ago, Mothers Against Drunk Driving was just beginning to make its anger felt, and drunk driving was still seen as a forgivable lapse of judgment, not deserving of severe chastisement. Only a few years ago one of the authors interviewed a construction worker who had accumulated ten drunk driving arrests, each one in a different state (because he moved from one construction job to another). He had never lost his license, nor had he paid any more than minor fines. Today he would be raked over some very hot coals.

For teens and parents, we have emphasized the necessity to reach an agreement and sign SADD's Contract for Life. We urge our readers, young or old, to always arrange in advance for a designated driver whenever drinking is likely; otherwise take a cab or bum a ride home. In the delightful 1989 film *Say Anything*, a sensitive story about teenagers, some scenes depict a party where the main character has been appointed "keymaster." He must remain sober, hold onto the car keys of everyone at the party, and not release them unless the driver is capable of driving safely or someone else takes that responsible role. Maybe there is something to be learned here. We think the change about drinking and driving is clear: drunk driving will not longer be tolerated and those who violate that rule will be treated harshly.

INTOXICATION AND EXPECTATION

One of the most intriguing discoveries to come out of alcohol research in the past decade involves a large number of studies, all of which lead to the same conclusion: alcohol alone is not the cause of "drunken behavior." Alcohol itself generates little more than a fuzzy experience of altered consciousness and impaired coordination. It does not automatically produce fistfights, amorous advances, maudlin sentimentality, or uncontrollable impulsiveness. The actual behavior of persons after drinking is the result of an interaction between several factors. These include what they *believe* will happen when they drink and what they think will be tolerated by others, as well as personality and genetic factors. If we believe that drinking leads to fighting, we may very well get into a fight. If we think alcohol produces a surge of sex hormones, we are likely to feel and act very sexy. In other words, it is not alcohol itself that produces intoxicated behavior. *Society* has a major effect on behavior by letting it be known how individuals can expect to feel and behave when they drink. The individual internalizes society's beliefs and expectancies for what is and is not OK to do while intoxicated, what will be tolerated and perhaps even excused, and what will not. Even long-term alcoholics, when given only tonic water while being told it is vodka and tonic, experience a reduction in craving for alcohol and relief of the "shakes." College students who erroneously think they are drinking vodka will become more aggressive or amorous or emotional even though they actually drink no alcohol at all. What would happen if college students believe that other students are much more accepting of drunkenness than they really are, and drink more than they should? Such mistaken beliefs were actually found in a large-scale study at a major university. Could these beliefs foster a self-fulfilling prophecy and promote unhealthy drinking habits?

In Germany beer can be purchased in many movie theaters and in all McDonald's restaurants. In giant German beer gardens, including those in the inner city, literally thousands of people, shoulder to shoulder, quaff liter-sized steins of beer as part of daily life. To accommodate those who want an added BA boost, women with trays of schnapps (hard liquor) circulate through the aisles to pour as many shots as the drinkers want. Nearly everyone drinks and a great many people become quite intoxicated. This includes a cross-section of German society such as families with children, military personnel, old people, teenagers and all social classes. The amazing thing to Americans is that there is almost never an incident of hostility or aggression despite all the drunkenness. Everyone behaves! It is understood in Germany that no matter how intoxicated you become, antisocial behavior is not permitted. Singing, laughing and a general sense of jubilant boisterousness prevail, but no misbehavior. How do you suppose thousands of intoxicated Americans would act in the same setting? Americans expect heavy drinking to cause undesirable behavior, including hostility, blatant sexual advances, and sometimes physical aggression or other acting out of impulses that are ordinarily restrained. Since Americans have such different expectations about acceptable behavior while drinking, it is no surprise that we do not have anything in our cities resembling the large German beer gardens. Here they probably wouldn't be as much fun and might in fact be hazardous to our health.

We know that children acquire their expectations about the effects of alcohol long before they try it, and that these early expectancies actually can serve as predictors of later adolescent drinking behavior, and perhaps even the risk of alcohol abuse in adulthood. Teen alcohol abusers are more likely than non-abusers to expect positive effects when they drink. These kids tend to believe that after drinking they will actually be *better* able to think and better coordinated than when sober. In addition, if they expect to receive social approval from other teens for drinking, they are more likely to drink. It is not surprising that teens who believe alcohol to be a magic elixir, one that will make them approved, competent and capable, are more prone to have problems with alcohol abuse as they get older.

So what does all this suggest? It raises the exciting possibility that if a culture can change its shared expectations about what happens when people drink, it can change its members' drinking habits and behavior when under the influence. We must let people of all ages know that drinking does *not* produce aggressive behavior, sexual boorishness or emotional outbursts on its own and that whether drinking or not we are all personally responsible for our own behavior. In short, we must let drinkers know that drinking alcohol can no longer be used as an excuse for undesirable behavior or anything else. Studies on the effects of alcohol expectations raise some other related questions, such as what actually happens when we get high, how does a sense of intoxication occur just because we *think* we had alcohol when we didn't and what potentials lie yet untapped in the realm of "natural highs" that occur without alcohol or drugs?

BLOOD ALCOHOL SCREENING

We recently were confronted by a strategically placed breath analyzing machine at the exit of a restaurant. All one had to do was put in a quarter, blow in a straw and get a blood alcohol reading. The front of the machine had a statement saying that the management was concerned about the safety of its patrons and urged them to check their BA and avoid driving if it was elevated. In the future such machines will be more and more in evidence— eventually they probably will be required by law in every bar in the country, as well they should be. You may also see blood alcohol machines appearing at places of employment. Although there are legitimate concerns about various civic rights issues involved in urine or blood sampling for routine drug testing, the use of a breath device to test for alcohol seems to us to be a different matter. It is in no way a humiliating as urine sampling might be, nor is it as frightening or as painful as a blood test. The breath test takes only 10 seconds. Is it an invasion of privacy? Maybe. But do individuals have the private right to have alcohol in their bloodstream while at work? A breath test is quick, can easily be performed on arrival at the workplace, and gives instant information about one's ability to perform. It certainly does not sound to us like too much to ask of those who work in situations where others' lives might depend on their sobriety.

At the time of this writing there is still no Federal Aviation Administration (FAA) requirement that airline pilots or copilots have their breath tested before a flight, nor are they even required to be tested immediately following an accident! Yet jockeys at our local racetracks must pass a breathalyzer test before they can ride a sulky behind a trotter. Does this make sense to you? If an airline can carefully inspect passengers' bags for dangerous objects, why shouldn't the blood alcohol of pilots be checked before they are allowed in the cockpit? Ideally, it would also be a good idea to test pilots for hangover effects since they too impair abilities involved in flying.

Just recently the pilot, copilot and flight engineer of a major airline were fired for flying under the influence of alcohol. Even though suspected of unsafe blood alcohol levels, their BAs were not tested *before* their early morning flight, but afterwards. These three flight personnel were suspected of flying while intoxicated because they had been observed by a number of bar patrons the previous evening drinking seven pitchers of beer and 19 mixed drinks between them! (Not only that, but their defense attorney argued that the pilot was an alcoholic and therefore tolerant to alcohol, so it wasn't a problem for him to fly after several drinks.)

We contacted the FAA and learned that there is no plan currently under consideration to require routine blood alcohol tests for airline flight crews, although government agencies are at least taking a preliminary look at the whole question of BA testing for transportation industry workers. Clearly the heavy-drinking crew described above should have been tested before their flight when it became widely known that they were at risk. We think it is inevitable that eventually all bus drivers, airline pilots, surgeons, air traffic controllers, truckers, police, heavy-equipment operators and other high-risk professionals will be required to begin their workshift with a puff into a breathalyzer. Those unwilling to be tested might have to consider alternative occupations.

Blood alcohol screening devices may also become part of routine driving. Cars belonging to convicted drunk drivers are already being equipped with breath analyzing devices that shut down the car's ignition if alcohol is detected. Designing security controls for such systems is difficult, but tamper-proof systems are currently under development. One example is an ignition switch that flashes five numbers in sequence when you turn it on; you are allowed five seconds to punch the numbers into a display board. If you cannot remember them, the ignition gives you a second try, then becomes inoperative for a programmed period.

Unfortunately, individual use of hand-held BA devices has not progressed as we predicted a decade ago because, unlike digital watches and other electronic devices, the price of breath testers has remained high. We expected to see digital personal breath testers available in the 1990s for under $30, but it hasn't happened. Digital units still cost over $300, putting them beyond the reach or practical consideration of the general public. We have seen "redlight-yellowlight-greenlight" models sold for as low as $39.95, but they tend to be unreliable and provide only minimal information. We hope someone will develop a low-cost breathalyzer during this decade so that by the turn of the century every drinker will be able to purchase one and have ready access to the invaluable information it provides.

LABELING ON BEVERAGE CONTAINERS

Labeling is coming. Producers of alcoholic beverages certainly do not want to have their products plastered with government-mandated health warnings and cautionary information. Yet it seems to us that the enjoyment of any product is not seriously compromised by providing information about its safe and proper use. Why should this not apply to alcohol? A simple statement about equivalency of different forms of alcohol would be helpful, such as, "This beer contains the same quantity of alcohol as a 4 oz. glass of table wine or a 1 1/4 oz. shot of hard liquor." An amount warning could be short and sweet:

Amount of Beer and Approximate BA for Males

(Female BAs slightly higher)

If you weigh 120 pounds and drink for an hour:
1 can = 0.15 BA; 2 cans = 0.45 BA; 3 cans = 0.80 BA.

If you weigh 170 pounds and drink for an hour:
2 cans = 0.30 BA; 3 cans = 0.50 BA; 4 cans = 0.70 BA.

After drinking for an hour you should only consume one drink per hour to avoid reaching BA levels significantly higher than those shown above.

Similar messages could appear on hard liquor bottles listing the effects of increasing numbers of shots and on wine bottles for glasses of wine. The government health information label could simply be included on all bottles and cans so the information would not crowd or interfere with the normal company brand and beverage labels.

MEDIA PORTRAYAL OF ALCOHOL

In studies analyzing the portrayal of drinking on television going back to the mid-1970s, it has been found that alcoholic beverages are by far the most frequently depicted. During the past two decades the frequency of drinking scenes actually seems to have increased, with more than ten acts of drinking occurring *per hour*, including situations with people drinking, fixing a drink, having a drink sitting nearby, or ordering drinks. It is curious that while in the real world alcoholic beverages account for only 16 percent of all beverages used, in the world of television they account of 74 percent of the beverages shown. Studies of British television programs reflect the same pattern, with drinking scenes very common (but rarely involving abuse or any health problems), featuring middle- and upper-class drinkers in generally positive or even luxurious settings. Most of the scenes depicting alcohol use include it as an incidental part of the situation and not a major feature of the scene. In any case, alcoholic beverages are now something of a standard "prop" on the television stage, having become "ubiquitous and taken for granted on television" *(Alcohol and Health, 1990)*. What effects might such a distorted portrayal of alcoholic beverage consumption have on children and adults? No clear evidence has yet demonstrated that it actually causes an increase in drinking, but it would seem that in terms of the expectancies described previously, if drinking is believed to occur almost everywhere and is a routine part of "the good life," one might be more inclined to drink. And if viewers see a great many drinking situations with primarily positive portrayals, rarely suggesting anything negative (only about 1 percent of situations portray abuse or health problems), then they might very well expect to enjoy drinking and perhaps even imagine having some kind of personal immunity to problems stemming from its use.

Films have become more responsible about alcohol in recent years, the hard-drinking hero or heroine having become passé, but alcohol remains a common feature in movies. Many scenes still take place in drinking settings such as bars, restaurants or resorts.

Media portrayals, from TV to films to magazine advertisements, pose a problem because we live in a free enterprise democracy where freedom of speech is cherished and censorship is abhorred. Nobody has the right or power to rule, "This is a glamorizing scene for alcohol. Take it out." Most of us are pleased that no one in our society can carry out such arbitrary censorship. Yet it would seem that some restraint is certainly warranted when dealing with a public health issue.

The essence of democratic coexistence is compromise, and that concept will no doubt prevail in relation to alcohol. In the future we will probably see less and less glamorization of drinking in films, on TV or in advertising, while alcoholic beverage producers will find ways to become comfortable with prominent government warnings and safe consumption notices on their products. The efforts to eliminate or markedly limit alcohol production and availability will fail, and probably should. The United States tried prohibition once and it was a sad failure that generated a whole new set of problems of its own.

Better education, realistic expectations for what alcohol will and will not do for drinkers, early intervention in drinking problems, and intense parental involvement in their childrens' drinking decisions are necessary to help society in its efforts to integrate public health needs with the reality of a drinking culture.

It is our hope that this book will make its own significant contribution as an aid to parents who are courageous enough to take on the vital task of providing basic alcohol education and guidance for their children. The need for this type of information is clearly apparent from the following facts:

- High school and junior high students drink 35 percent of all wine coolers sold in the United States and 1.1 billion cans of beer each year.

- In 1990 one out of four youths ages 12 to 13 had consumed alcohol. Ninety percent of seniors in high school have used alcohol.

- About 5.5 million junior and senior high school students have "binged" with five or more drinks in a row; 454,000 report weekly consumption of 15 drinks.

- In 1990, $752 million was spent on beer and wine advertising and $291 million was spent on distilled spirits advertising. A 1988 survey for the Bureau of Alcohol, Tobacco and Firearms found that 80 percent of Americans believe alcohol advertising influences underage youth to drink alcohol.

- Almost two-thirds of students who drink buy their own alcohol; 7 million students report being able to purchase alcohol in a store.

- Cisco, a fortified wine that contains 2.5 times more alcohol than other alcoholic beverages, was identified as non-alcoholic by 36 percent of students surveyed. Among students who drink, 42 percent prefer wine coolers.

- In 1990, among youths 12 to 17 years old, 52 percent of whites report having consumed alcohol, compared with 48 percent of Hispanics and 33 percent of blacks.

Sources: National Institute on Drug Abuse; U.S. Department of Health and Human Services, 1991.

References

Alberti,R., and M. Emmons. *Your Perfect Right*. San Louis Obispo, CA: Impact Publishers, 1988.

Banks, W.P., R.E. Vogler and T.A. Weissbach. Adaptation of ethanol intoxication. *Bulletin of the Psychonomic Society* 14:319-322, 1979.

Bartz, W.R. and R.A. Rasor. *Surviving with Kids*. San Louis Obispo, CA: Impact Publishers, 1978.

Benton, R.P. Does an Increase in Tolerance Cause an Increase in ad lib Consumption of Alcohol? Unpublished doctoral dissertation, Claremont Graduate School, Claremont, CA, 1983.

Benton, R.P., W.P. Banks and R.E. Vogler. Carryover of tolerance to alcohol in moderate drinkers. *Journal of Studies on Alcohol* 43:1127-1148, 1982.

Ford, G. *The Benefits of Moderate Drinking*. San Francisco: Wine Appreciation Guild, 1988.

Forgatch, M.S. and G.R. Patterson. *Parents and Adolescents Living Together. Parts 1 and 2*. Eugene, OR: Castalia Press, 1989.

Intoximeters, Inc. (makers of breath analysis devices), 1901 Locust Street, St. Louis, MO 63103; (314)241-1158.

Johnston, L.D., and P.M. O'Malley. Why do the nations's students use drugs and alcohol? Self-reported reasons from nine national surveys. *Journal of Drug Issues* 16(1):67-90,1986.

Markham, M.R. *The BACCuS Program* (computer program for estimating blood alcohol). Albuquerque:University of New Mexico Press, 1990.

Seventh Special Report to the U.S. Congress on Alcohol and Health (ADM 281-88-0002). Rockville, MD: U.S. Department of Health and Human Services, 1990.

Siegal, R. *Intoxication: Life in Pursuit of Artificial Paradise.* New York: E.P. Dutton, 1989.

Vaillant, G.E. *The Natural History of Alcoholism.* Cambridge, MA: Harvard University Press, 1983.

Vogler, R.E., and W.R. Bartz. *The Better Way to Drink.* Oakland, CA: New Harbinger Publications, 1982.

Vogler, R.E., and T.A. Weissbach and J.V. Compton. Learning techniques for alcohol abuse. *Behavior Research and Therapy* 15:31-38, 1977.

Webber, N.E. Development and reversal of tolerance from controlled changes in ethanol consumption. *Dissertation Abstracts International* 43(9):3049b, 1982 (University Microfilms No. ABG 83-02756).

Suggested Readings

Engs, R. *Alcohol and Other Drugs: Self-Responsibility.* Bloomington, IN: Tichenor Publishing, 1990.

Fingarette, H. *Heavy Drinking: The Myth of Alcoholism as a Disease.* Berkeley: University of California Press, 1988.

Heather, N. and I. Robertson. *Problem Drinking: The New Approach.* New York: Viking/Penguin, 1985.

Miller, W.R., and R.F. Munoz. *How to Control Your Drinking.* Albuquerque: University of New Mexico Press, 1982.

Peele, S. *The Diseasing of America: Addiction Treatment Out of Control.* Lexington, MA: Lexington Books, 1989.

Smith, M. *When I Say No I Feel Guilty.* New York: Dial Press, 1975.

APPENDIX

Weight, Drinks, and Blood Alcohol by Sex*

DRINK EQUIVALENTS

One Drink = 12 oz beer = 4 oz wine = 2 ½ oz fortified wine = 1 ¼ oz liquor

Note: Male and female blood alcohol figures are different and are presented separately. To make them easier to remember, BA figures are rounded to the nearest 5 or 0; for example, 58 = 60, 122 = 120 (or 0.058 = 0.060, 0.122 = 0.120).

80-pound Female

Hours Since Start of Drinking

Number of Drinks	1	2	3	4	5	6	7
1	40	25	10	0	0	0	0
2	95	80	65	50	3C	15	0
3	155	135	120	105	90	75	55
4	210	195	175	160	145	130	115
5	265	250	235	215	200	185	170
6	320	305	290	275	260	240	225
7	380	360	345	330	315	300	280
8	435	420	400	385	370	355	340
9	490	475	460	440	425	410	395
10	545	530	514	498	482	465	450

* These tables were derived and modified from the BACCuS program, a computer program developed by Michael R. Markham of the University of New Mexico, Albuquerque, in 1988. Our special thanks to Professor William R. Miller.

100-pound Female

Hours Since Start of Drinking

Number of Drinks	1	2	3	4	5	6	7
1	30	15	0	0	0	0	0
2	75	60	40	25	10	0	0
3	120	105	85	70	55	40	25
4	165	150	130	115	100	85	70
5	210	195	175	160	145	130	115
6	255	240	220	205	190	175	160
7	300	285	265	250	235	220	205
8	345	330	310	295	280	265	250
9	390	375	355	340	325	310	295
10	435	420	400	385	370	355	340

120-pound Female

Hours Since Start of Drinking

Number of Drinks	1	2	3	4	5	6	7
1	20	5	0	0	0	0	0
2	60	45	25	10	0	0	0
3	95	80	65	50	35	15	0
4	135	120	100	85	70	55	40
5	170	155	140	125	110	90	75
6	210	195	175	160	145	130	115
7	245	230	215	200	185	165	150
8	285	270	250	235	220	205	190
9	320	305	290	275	260	240	225
10	360	345	325	310	295	280	265

140-pound Female

Hours Since Start of Drinking

Number of Drinks	1	2	3	4	5	6	7
1	15	0	0	0	0	0	0
2	50	30	15	0	0	0	0
3	80	65	50	30	15	0	0
4	115	95	80	65	50	35	15
5	145	130	115	95	80	65	50
6	175	160	145	130	115	95	80
7	210	195	175	160	145	130	115
8	240	225	210	195	175	160	145
9	275	255	240	225	210	195	175
10	305	290	275	255	240	225	210

160-pound Female

Hours Since Start of Drinking

Number of Drinks	1	2	3	4	5	6	7
1	10	0	0	0	0	0	0
2	40	25	10	0	0	0	0
3	70	50	35	20	5	0	0
4	95	80	65	50	30	15	0
5	125	110	95	75	60	45	30
6	155	135	120	105	90	75	55
7	180	165	150	135	115	100	85
8	210	195	175	160	145	130	115
9	235	220	205	190	175	155	140
10	265	250	235	215	200	185	170

180-pound Female

Hours Since Start of Drinking

Number of Drinks	1	2	3	4	5	6	7
1	10	0	0	0	0	0	0
2	35	20	0	0	0	0	0
3	60	45	25	10	0	0	0
4	85	70	50	35	20	5	0
5	110	95	75	60	45	30	15
6	135	120	100	85	70	55	40
7	160	145	125	110	95	80	65
8	185	170	150	135	120	105	90
9	210	195	175	160	145	130	115
10	235	220	200	185	170	155	140

200-pound Female

Hours Since Start of Drinking

Number of Drinks	1	2	3	4	5	6	7
1	5	0	0	0	0	0	0
2	30	15	0	0	0	0	0
3	50	35	20	5	0	0	0
4	75	60	40	25	10	0	0
5	95	80	65	50	35	15	0
6	120	105	85	70	55	40	25
7	140	125	110	95	80	60	45
8	165	150	130	115	100	85	70
9	185	170	155	140	125	105	90
10	210	195	175	160	145	130	115

100-pound Male

Hours Since Start of Drinking

Number of Drinks	1	2	3	4	5	6	7
1	20	5	0	0	0	0	0
2	60	45	25	10	0	0	0
3	95	80	65	50	35	15	0
4	135	120	100	85	70	55	40
5	170	155	140	125	110	90	75
6	210	195	175	160	145	130	115
7	245	230	215	200	185	165	150
8	285	270	250	235	220	205	190
9	320	305	290	275	260	240	225
10	360	345	325	310	295	280	265

120-pound Male

Hours Since Start of Drinking

Number of Drinks	1	2	3	4	5	6	7
1	15	0	0	0	0	0	0
2	45	30	15	0	0	0	0
3	80	60	45	30	15	0	0
4	110	95	75	60	45	30	15
5	140	125	110	90	75	60	45
6	170	155	140	125	110	90	75
7	205	185	170	155	140	125	105
8	235	220	200	185	170	155	140
9	265	250	235	215	200	185	170
10	295	280	265	250	230	215	200

140-pound Male

Hours Since Start of Drinking

Number of Drinks	1	2	3	4	5	6	7
1	10	0	0	0	0	0	0
2	40	20	5	0	0	0	0
3	65	50	30	15	0	0	0
4	90	75	60	45	25	10	0
5	120	100	85	70	55	40	20
6	145	130	115	95	80	65	50
7	170	155	140	125	110	90	75
8	200	180	165	150	135	120	100
9	225	210	195	175	160	145	130
10	250	235	220	205	190	170	155

160-pound Male

Hours Since Start of Drinking

Number of Drinks	1	2	3	4	5	6	7
1	5	0	0	0	0	0	0
2	30	15	0	0	0	0	0
3	55	40	20	5	0	0	0
4	80	60	45	30	15	0	0
5	100	85	70	55	35	20	5
6	125	110	95	75	60	45	30
7	150	130	115	100	85	70	50
8	170	155	140	125	110	90	75
9	195	180	165	145	130	115	100
10	220	200	185	170	155	140	120

180-pound Male

Hours Since Start of Drinking

Number of Drinks	1	2	3	4	5	6	7
1	5	0	0	0	0	0	0
2	25	10	0	0	0	0	0
3	45	30	15	0	0	0	0
4	65	50	35	20	5	0	0
5	90	70	55	40	25	10	0
6	110	95	75	60	45	30	15
7	130	115	100	80	65	50	35
8	150	135	120	105	85	70	55
9	170	155	140	125	110	90	75
10	190	175	160	145	130	110	95

200-pound Male

Hours Since Start of Drinking

Number of Drinks	1	2	3	4	5	6	7
1	5	0	0	0	0	0	0
2	20	5	0	0	0	0	0
3	40	25	10	0	0	0	0
4	60	45	25	10	0	0	0
5	80	60	45	30	15	0	0
6	95	80	65	50	35	15	0
7	115	100	85	65	50	35	20
8	135	120	100	85	70	55	40
9	155	135	120	105	90	75	55
10	170	155	140	125	110	90	75

220-pound Male

Hours Since Start of Drinking

Number of Drinks	1	2	3	4	5	6	7
1	0	0	0	0	0	0	0
2	20	0	0	0	0	0	0
3	35	20	5	0	0	0	0
4	50	35	20	5	0	0	0
5	70	55	35	20	5	0	0
6	85	70	55	40	20	5	0
7	105	85	70	55	40	25	5
8	120	105	90	70	55	40	25
9	135	120	105	90	75	55	40
10	155	140	120	105	90	75	60

240-pound Male

Hours Since Start of Drinking

Number of Drinks	1	2	3	4	5	6	7
1	0	0	0	0	0	0	0
2	15	0	0	0	0	0	0
3	30	15	0	0	0	0	0
4	45	30	15	0	0	0	0
5	60	45	30	15	0	0	0
6	80	60	45	30	15	0	0
7	95	75	60	45	30	15	0
8	110	95	75	60	45	30	15
9	125	110	95	75	60	45	30
10	140	125	110	90	75	60	45

260-pound Male

Hours Since Start of Drinking

Number of Drinks	1	2	3	4	5	6	7
1	0	0	0	0	0	0	0
2	15	0	0	0	0	0	0
3	25	10	0	0	0	0	0
4	40	25	10	0	0	0	0
5	55	40	25	10	0	0	0
6	70	55	40	25	5	0	0
7	85	70	55	35	20	5	0
8	100	85	65	50	35	20	5
9	115	100	80	65	50	35	20
10	130	110	95	80	65	50	30

280-pound Male

Hours Since Start of Drinking

Number of Drinks	1	2	3	4	5	6	7
1	0	0	0	0	0	0	0
2	10	0	0	0	0	0	0
3	25	10	0	0	0	0	0
4	40	20	5	0	0	0	0
5	50	35	20	5	0	0	0
6	65	50	30	15	0	0	0
7	80	60	45	30	15	0	0
8	90	75	60	45	25	10	0
9	105	90	75	55	40	25	10
10	120	100	85	70	55	40	20